T0330968

Routledge Revivals

Paciolo on Accounting

Paciolo on Accounting

R. GENE BROWN
KENNETH S. JOHNSTON

Routledge
Taylor & Francis Group

First published in 1963 by McGraw-Hill Book Company, Inc.

This edition first published in 2018 by Routledge
2 Park Square, Milton Park, Abingdon, Oxon, OX14 4RN
and by Routledge
52 Vanderbilt Avenue, New York, NY 10017, USA

Routledge is an imprint of the Taylor & Francis Group, an informa business

© 1963 by Taylor and Francis

Publisher's Note
The publisher has gone to great lengths to ensure the quality of this reprint but points out that some imperfections in the original copies may be apparent.

Disclaimer
The publisher has made every effort to trace copyright holders and welcomes correspondence from those they have been unable to contact.
A Library of Congress record exists under ISBN:

ISBN 13: 978-0-367-17931-1 (hbk)
ISBN 13: 978-0-429-05852-3 (ebk)

Paciolo on Accounting

Paciolo on Accounting

R. GENE BROWN, PH.D., CPA
Graduate School of Business
Stanford University

KENNETH S. JOHNSTON, PH.D.
Graduate School of Business Administration
Northwestern University

With an Introduction by
ALVIN R. JENNINGS, CPA *Executive Partner*
Lybrand, Ross Bros. & Montgomery

McGraw-Hill Book Company, Inc.
New York, San Francisco, Toronto, London
1963

Library of Congress Catalog Card Number: 63-20051

08477

ABOUT THE COVER. The color scheme which appears on the cover is essentially the same as appears on the 1494 edition of Paciolo's SUMMA. The geometric design, a polyhedron, is a replica of the crystal which hangs from the ceiling in the painting of Paciolo reproduced in this book. Drawings of such polyhedrons are found throughout the SUMMA, for a major part of it is devoted to arithmetic and geometry. Paciolo frequently constructed similar crystals for use in lectures and exhibitions.

The cover of this book was designed by Mr. Gartner Ertman, Koch and Associates, Architects.

Design & composition by Capital City Press with printing by Halliday Lithograph in the United States of America

TO
HECTOR R. ANTON

"... may it be accessible to everyone, so that our country may, through the instrumentality of language, be enriched in these disciplines ..."

Luca Paciolo in the dedication
of his revision of Campanus'
edition of Euclid.
Venice, June 5, 1509.

Contents

Introduction

The historian often transcends the events which he chronicles. In this sense he shares the art of the conductor who, by his genius, enhances the score. Beethoven is *latent* beauty; Beethoven plus a Toscanini or an Ormandy *is* beauty.

Fr. Luca Paciolo, mistakenly, often is referred to as the originator of double-entry bookkeeping. The fact is that we don't know who the originator was. His identity remains a mystery. Not so with Paciolo whose SUMMA so captured the imagination and interest of scholars of accounting that it has been translated into Dutch, Italian, German, French and Russian as well as English.

Can any of us ignore a personality who, almost five centuries ago realized that theory was valueless unless it could be put to practical use; who recognized that the truth was fundamental to a sound system of accounts; who appreciated that character was the only sound basis for credit; who fully realized the importance of internal control; who warned against those who "keep their books in duplicate, showing one to the buyer and the other to the seller;" who advocated auditing and who warned of the pitfalls in dealing with governmental agencies?

A sense of historical perspective is evidence of maturity of professions as well as of individuals. No man can truly understand his own profession until he is capable of relating it to the past, the present and the future.

Every student who wishes to master accounting, every teacher who aspires to instruct in the subject, every practicing accountant who professes to understand his discipline should read this interpretation of the significance of Paciolo and his work.

ALVIN R. JENNINGS

Preface

Accounting has a rich heritage, as do many other professions. It has evolved in much the same way as common law, responding to business needs which arise with changes in language and techniques. However, it is remarkable that the basic framework of the double entry process, which has existed over 500 years, remains unchanged. Today, manipulation of data within accounting systems takes place at unbelievable speeds, but the double entry system of bookkeeping still encompasses these and other "modern" accounting developments.

This book is about Luca Paciolo and his extraordinary contribution to the development of the accounting profession. Paciolo is the first known writer to publish a work describing the double entry process. This publication appeared in the form of a treatise included in the SUMMA DE ARITHMETICA, GEOMETRIA, PROPORTIONI ET PROPORTIONALITA, published in Venice in 1494. It is undoubtedly the most famous accounting work ever to be printed. Many paragraphs of Paciolo's work could be inserted into current textbooks and articles with little more than slight wording changes. The "principles" and "rules" for bookkeeping suggested in the treatise are applicable to much of modern accounting practice.

Unfortunately, this most famous work is also extremely rare. Because of this, few accountants have had the opportunity to examine the book. Mrs. Dorothea Reeves, Curator of the Kress Library at the Graduate School of Business Administration of Harvard University, gave us our initial opportunity to examine both the first and second editions of the SUMMA. It was this contact, together with an interest in accounting history stimulated while graduate students at the University of California at Berkeley, that led directly to the publication of this book.

Literature is better appreciated and understood if one knows something about the author. Therefore, the introductory section of this book tells about the significance of Paciolo's work, his childhood and adolescence, and his scholarly pursuits as a mature intellectual. The social and economic atmosphere which shaped his character is also discussed. A modernized translation, a photo-offset reproduction of the original, and a bibliography follow the first section.

There were two problems in particular which confronted us in writing this book. First, much of what is written must necessarily be interpretive, yet be presented in line with all available facts. Second, an attempt must be made to achieve the proper balance between a sterile reiteration of facts, and a lively, but vacuous, discussion. To satisfy these criteria, we were compelled to break away from the outmoded linguistics of the original, and to recast Paciolo in contemporary English. The greatest danger in this is that the "flavor" of the original will be lost. We have strived to retain this original flavor, and still make Paciolo's treatise easy to read.

There have been two translations of Paciolo in the twentieth century, one by Pietro Crivelli in 1924, and the other by John B. Geijsbeek in 1914. Crivelli's translation attempted to adhere faithfully to the original, while Geijsbeek tried to provide a more readable translation. In addition to using contemporary English, our translation tries to clarify some old ambiguities.

A special note of thanks is due Mrs. Reeves of the Kress Library and Mr. Lawrence J. Kipp, the librarian of Baker Library, Harvard University, for their encouragement in this project and for the permission to use both the original and second editions of Paciolo for preparation of the photo-offset plates. In addition to this, Mrs. Reeves provided much technical assistance. We are also indebted to those who typed the many drafts of the manuscripts, Ann Brown, Jill Halliday, and Ruth Davis.

In his writing and teaching, Paciolo continuously attempted to make what he had to say interesting to many people, and not just the scholars of his field. Our overriding objectives correspond to his: First, to make this work available to many, and second, to provide a scholarly work that can be read and enjoyed.

R. Gene Brown
Kenneth S. Johnston

Luca Paciolo and his friend, Guidobaldo, Duke of Urbino.

The Painting of Paciolo

The picture reproduced in this book is a photograph of the famous painting of Paciolo which hangs in the Naples National Museum. For many years there was considerable uncertainty concerning the identity of the artist. It is now generally conceded that the artist was Jacopo de Barbari. The Superintendent of the Naples National Museum, Mr. Gino Doria, wrote us about the unknown painter as follows:

> . . . this painting is signed, Jaco. Bar Vigennis. P. 1495, a painter who remains unknown, which cannot be; because of chronology and stylistic character it has been suggested that it was Jacopo de Barbari. It is thought the unknown Jaco. Bar. was a Venetian, and perhaps a follower of Piero della Francesca in the Urbino environment.

In addition to the early uncertainty about the painter, some writers have incorrectly claimed that the book which is open and to which Paciolo is pointing, is a copy of his Summa. This is doubtful for two reasons. First, the Summa is a much larger book than that opened in front of Paciolo. It may well be that the larger book to Paciolo's left, which is closed with clasps, is the Summa. Second, the book under Paciolo's left hand is open at Chapter 13, entitled Euclid. The Summa does not have a Chapter 13 devoted to Euclid.

It is easy to understand why some writers misinterpreted this painting, for Paciolo once referred to a painting which depicts him holding the Summa. Taylor, in No Royal Road, identifies Paciolo in "The Virgin and Child and Saints," painted by Paciolo's friend, Piero della Francesca. This painting, which is in the Pinacoteca of Perugia, shows Paciolo holding a heavy book which has approximately the same dimensions and binding of the SUMMA's that we have examined. This is undoubtedly the painting to which Paciolo was referring.

Taylor describes his reaction to the painting by de Barbari as follows:

> As one sees this picture where it hangs near a door in the large room of the Naples Museum, he is struck first by the stern, serious, determined face of Paciolo, circled by the hood of the order, and with the striking contrast of flesh color and the gray-green tinge of his habit upon which the light plays. The whole background of the picture is black. The table is green, the frame of the slate ordinary wood color, the open book cover blue. The young man wears a black biretta, a black fur-lined coat, a red undergarment showing at the throat and above the elbows, and gloves. Both men have blue eyes. The picture measures about five feet wide and four feet high. Apparently it has been many times redone. The picture is on canvas on wood and contains several worm holes. It has been much damaged but has been creditably restored.
>
> ... on a small scrap of paper on the table is the inscription "Jaco. Bar. Vigennis, P. 149(?)" The exact year is burned out and it appears that a five has been inserted. Upon the book which may be the SUMMA, is a wood polyhedron. From the ceiling at the left is suspended a crystal prism.

This is the crystal prism which is imprinted on the cover of this book.

SECTION I

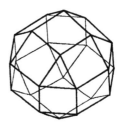

Paciolo: The Man, His Work

Paciolo: The Man, His Work

Most accounting books published today make some reference to Luca Paciolo's treatise on bookkeeping, published in 1494 in the SUMMA DE ARITHMETICA, GEOMETRIA, PROPORTIONI ET PROPORTIONALITA. At first glance, this might appear to result from some professional obsession with history, but this is not the case. The fact that Paciolo was the first author to publish on double entry bookkeeping is not the primary reason for such homage. On the contrary, it is because the basic framework for the double entry process detailed by Paciolo has remained unchanged for almost 500 years. Most of the accounting methodology suggested in the treatise, as well as Paciolo's suggestions on how to succeed in business, are as applicable today as they were in the 15th century.

Along with his peers, Piero della Francesca, Leon Battista Alberti, Federigo the Duke of Urbino, Leonardo da Vinci, Leonardo da Pisa, Raphael, and Michelangelo, Paciolo typified the "all purpose" man of the Golden Age of the Renaissance. In fact, all of these men except the last two mentioned, were friends of Paciolo. Just as are Leonardo da Vinci's works studied and revered today, so are those of Luca Paciolo.

Although Paciolo's work in his many areas of interest is universally respected, as an individual he has been the center of controversy for years. At various times he has been called a religious mystic as well as a heretic; a traditionalist as well as an iconoclast; an outgoing friend of students as well as a recluse; a brilliant individualist as well as an opportunist; an original scholar as well as a plagiarist. Although a personal friend of seven successive Popes, starting with Paul II in 1464 and ending about 50 years later with Sixtus IV, Paciolo was once threatened with excommunication by the Franciscan Order which he had joined in the 1470's.

3

We are convinced that Paciolo was an excellent writer, a spellbinding lecturer and teacher, a deeply religious man, and an acknowledged scholar in mathematics, theology, architecture, military strategy, sports and games, and the world of business. During his career he taught at five universities, Florence, Milan, Perugia, Naples and Rome. He also served as a private tutor in courts and for various wealthy families.

On the other hand, we have concluded that although religious, Paciolo was not very sensitive to the responsibilities of his Franciscan brotherhood. Although scholarly, he was primarily a compiler and translator rather than a developer and expositor of new theorems. Paciolo felt that theory was important, but was useless if it could not be put to practical use. Further, most books in the early 15th century were written in Latin. Because of this, they were available only to the scholars of the time. By writing in the "vulgar" tongue, Paciolo concerned himself with communicating knowledge to the people. It was to this end that he devoted most of his teaching and literary career. Applying mathematical concepts and techniques to the business community, and writing about them in the vernacular, represented a great contribution. The widespread use of Paciolo's published works, as well as his reputation as a lecturer and teacher, bore ample testimony to his success.

Never does Paciolo claim to be an originator. In the treatise on bookkeeping, for example, Paciolo states that ". . . the system employed in Venice will be adopted here, for it is certainly recommended above all others."

In 1878, the people of Borgo San Sepolcro erected a plaque in commemoration of Paciolo which translates as follows:[1]

> To Luca Pacioli, who was friend and advisor to Leonardo da Vinci and Leon Battista Alberti, and who first gave to algebra the voice and structure of a science. He was the great founder of its ap-

[1] The reader will notice that the plaque uses the spelling "Pacioli" rather than "Paciolo." The exact spelling of his name has been the subject of some controversy. On page 76 of the January 1944 issue of the ACCOUNTING REVIEW, Taylor comments on this problem as follows:

"Those who care to use the Latin correctly write "Lucas Paciolus;" those who care to follow the singular in the Italian are perfectly correct in spelling the name "Paciolo;" those who prefer to follow usage and a practice which is very general in many fields, are correct in spelling the name "Pacioli." It is wholly a matter of choosing to follow form or usage; but this is an old controversy which is never

plication to geometry. He invented double entry bookkeeping and wrote mathematical works which became the foundation and unvaried form for future thinking.

At the instigation of their Society of Commercial Workers, and shamed by 370 years of forgetfulness, the people of San Sepolcro have erected this plaque to their great citizen. 1878.

Of course, Paciolo did not invent double entry bookkeeping, for there is evidence of its existence as early as the beginning of the 14th century. Nevertheless, by becoming the first author to write of it, and to do so in the common tongue, Paciolo earned the title, "The Father of Accounting."

The environment in which Paciolo worked during the Renaissance, the influence of many of his friends on his work, and the many activities and interests he had, make a fascinating history. After discussing the nature and significance of his work, we should like to tell something of this history. Following this, we will present a new translation of his bookkeeping treatise and a reproduction of the original publication itself.

The Author

Paciolo was a prolific writer. From an outline of his various literary efforts, the breadth of his interests can be appreciated. In chronological order, he is thought to have written the following:

1) 1470 A manuscript on algebra. This manuscript was dedicated to Paciolo's pupils, the sons of the wealthy Venetian merchant, Rompiasi. It has been lost. However, it is likely that it was subsequently incorporated in the SUMMA published in 1494.

---

settled. My choice is "Pacioli;" but any other spelling that anyone cares to use will be all right with me."

We prefer to stay free from this controversy, tending to agree with Professor Raymond de Roover, writing in the same issue of the ACCOUNTING REVIEW, page 69:

"Since it is impossible to settle the question at issue from the available evidence, it should be permissable to use either "Paciolo" or "Pacioli" . . . As a matter of expediency, it might be desirable to reach an agreement among scholars and to avoid confusion by adopting a uniform spelling, Paciolo in preference to Pacioli."

2) 1476 A manuscript on regular bodies. This manuscript covered algebra and the five regular bodies in geometry, and was dedicated to the youths of Perugia. It was unpublished as such and is now in the Vatican Library in Rome. It is possible that this is a translation of a work done on the same subject by Paciolo's friend, Piero della Francesca. Most of Paciolo's early unpublished manuscripts were later incorporated in whole or in part into his SUMMA or the DIVINA; this one was no exception.

3) 1480 A manuscript on Euclid's geometry. There is some doubt that this manuscript ever existed. Even if it did, the exact nature of the subject matter would be unknown. The reason for suspecting its existence is that Paciolo says he did a manuscript about this time. There is also a reference in a Vatican manuscript to the effect that in December 1480, a Brother Anthony received a copy of a book on Euclid from Luca Paciolo in Perugia. It is quite possible that this was Paciolo's translation of Euclid's work into Italian. It is reasonably certain that Paciolo did translate Euclid into Italian, but this manuscript has also been lost.

4) 1481 A manuscript on algebra. This was the manuscript which Paciolo composed at Zara. It is probably similar to the works previously done in Perugia and in Venice, but was an independent effort. It has been lost.

5) 1494 SUMMA DE ARITHMETICA, GEOMETRIA, PROPORTIONI ET PROPORTIONALITA. This is probably Paciolo's most famous published work and is the book containing the bookkeeping treatise, "De Computis et Scripturis." It was published in Venice.

6) 1504 LA SCUOLA PERFETTA DEI MERCANTI. This was a reprint of the bookkeeping section of the SUMMA and was published in Toscolano by Paganini, the individual who printed the original SUMMA.

7) 1505 SCHIFANOIA. This book contained mathematical games and chess problems. It is thought to have been published in Florence. It has been lost.

8) 1508 DE VIRIBUS QUANTITATIS. This book contains a discussion of numerical powers, geometry, and a collection of mathematical games. A copy is in the library of the University of Bologna.

9) 1509 DE DIVINA PROPORTIONE. This is the second major book which Paciolo published. It was published in Venice, containing

240 pages, and was printed by hand. Leonardo da Vinci and Paciolo collaborated on this book. The Divina was Paciolo's most scholarly effort. In the first chapter of the Divina, Paciolo argues that ". . . without a knowledge of mathematical sciences no good work is possible," and the book is devoted to an examination of the applied "mathematical sciences." It contained three sections: The first on arithmetic, geometry, and proportion; the second on the architecture of holy temples, places that serve health, the defense of states and private houses; the third, a treatise on regular bodies of geometry.

10) 1509 CAMPANUS' EUCLID. This was a revision of Campanus' edition of Euclid and was translated into Latin by Paciolo. It was published in Venice.

11) 1523 SUMMA DE ARITHMETICA, GEOMETRIA, PROPORTIONI ET PROPORTIONALITA. This was the second edition of the original SUMMA published in 1494. This edition was published in Toscolano by Paganini. It is practically identical to the first.

We cannot be absolutely certain that those items "lost" were ever published. Nor can we be sure of the dates, even if they were. In fact, there is some doubt about whether a few of the items listed ever existed. Some writers have mentioned that Paciolo wrote a separate manuscript on architecture and one on the figures of the ancient characters in the alphabet. This is quite possible because both of these subjects are covered in the DIVINA. In any event, it can easily be seen that Paciolo's reputation as one of the "all purpose men" of the Renaissance is deserved.

Both of his major works, the SUMMA and the DIVINA, are world famous. Our primary concern is with the SUMMA DE ARITHMETICA, GEOMETRIA, PROPORTIONI ET PROPORTIONALITA, for it contains the treatise on bookkeeping.

In addition to a second edition of the SUMMA published in 1523, the bookkeeping section was deemed sufficiently important to have been reprinted as a separate unit in 1504. It was customary for the first editions of a book to have a sponsor underwrite the publishing costs. However, as testimony to the demand for these works, the publication of the bookkeeping treatise and the second edition was financed by Paganini, who originally printed the SUMMA in 1494.

7

Over the years there have been at least nine different translations of Paciolo's SUMMA in six languages: Dutch, Italian, German, French, Russian, and English. The first translation of Paciolo was by a Dutchman, Jan Ympyn Christoffels. Christoffels translated Paciolo into Dutch, French and English in 1543. The first German translation was in 1876, the first Russian translation in 1893. The translation included in this book is the fourth English translation of Paciolo, preceded by Christoffels in 1543, John Geijsbeek in 1914 and Pietro Crivelli in 1924. In preparing this translation, we have attempted to modernize the language of the treatise so that the reader is unencumbered by outmoded verbiage which adds nothing to the flavor of the original and, in fact, detracts from its readability.

Paciolo's objective in writing the SUMMA was to collect material on mathematics and bookkeeping and put it in the hands of the Italian people, hoping that they would use it to improve their lives. Paciolo has been called "The first experimentalist to put theory into practice."

The SUMMA contains five major sections: 1) arithmetic and algebra, 2) the use of arithmetic and algebra in trade and reckoning, 3) bookkeeping, 4) money and exchange, and 5) pure and applied geometry. Money necessary for the initial publication of the SUMMA was provided by Marco Sanuto, a professor of mathematics. It is said that the SUMMA was the most exhaustive and widely read mathematical work in the whole of Italy.

The section of bookkeeping was the only publication covering this subject until 1525, when a book was published by Giovanni Antonio Tagliente. However, it was not until 1534 that Domenico Manzoni published a popular book on the subject. This book went through six or seven editions. Manzoni's work was little more than a revision of Paciolo. Page after page is identical, except for the removal of religious expressions and personal observations characteristic of Paciolo's writings.

In his treatise, Paciolo says that he is describing the method used in Venice. Between the 12th and the 15th century, Venice was one of the most powerful and well developed republics in western Europe. It is not surprising, therefore, that Paciolo felt that the method of Venice was to be "recommended above all others." Undoubtedly, accounting evolved to satisfy the needs of burgeoning Venetian commerce, just as it has responded to business needs throughout the centuries.

8

The treatise on bookkeeping called, "Particularis de Computis et Scripturis," which translates "Details of Accounting and Recording," is divided into two principal parts: The first called Inventory and the second called Disposition. In these two parts Paciolo discusses in detail the bookkeeping process that we know today: Taking an inventory of the assets of a business; recording the original entries in the accounting records based on that inventory; recording business transactions; posting to the Ledger, complete with comments on posting references; preparing a trial balance to check the accuracy of the bookkeeping process; and closing the nominal accounts through profit and loss into the capital account.

In addition to the procedural aspects of the bookkeeping process, Paciolo was concerned with internal controls. He recommended that the Memorandum, Journal, and Ledger be numbered and dated, and that their pages be prenumbered. Among other things, he recommends that transaction documents be complete in detail, and permanently filed; that a summary account for small business expense be kept, arguing that separate accounts for miscellaneous expenditures would be too involved and expensive; and that the books be audited for internal check.

Although we have now abandoned the Memorandum as the book in which business transactions should be recorded chronologically, the overall process described by Paciolo is otherwise precisely the same as is now performed.

In addition to the interesting aspects of the accounting process, one is constantly reminded of his common touch. Some of the business proverbs cited in the bookkeeping treatise make interesting reading. For example, "Where there is no order there is chaos," "Every action is determined by the end in view," "One who does nothing makes no mistakes; one who makes no mistakes does not learn," "Officials do not bother with details," "He who does business without knowing all about it sees his money go like flies," and "Frequent accounting makes for lasting friendship."

Directly or indirectly through the Dutch and the English, Paciolo laid the foundation for our present accounting literature and our knowledge of bookkeeping. The so-called modern aspects of the accounting process are reflected largely by streamlined and sophisticated techniques for data collection, its processing, and the preparation of reports. Although one frequently finds expensive electronic equipment performing the accounting process, the entire structure governing these processes is the same as it was when Paciolo outlined it in 1494. Of course, it is possible that accountants will not always adhere to the double-entry process, but they have been doing so for almost 500 years.

A person's work is always better understood and appreciated if the conditions under which he worked, and something of the man himself, are known. Paciolo was not only an interesting individual, but lived during the most intellectually exciting fifty year period prior to the 20th century.

The Formative Years[2]

Although the exact date of Paciolo's birth is not known, the year 1445 is thought by many to be correct. As was indicated in the translation of the memorial plaque presented earlier, he was born in a small Italian town, Borgo San Sepolcro, which is about 80 miles southeast of Florence. If one could in some way remove the Lambrettas and Fiats from the streets, San Sepolcro would appear today much as it did in Paciolo's time. It is typical of many small Italian towns, being dominated by a large cathedral and a public square, and surrounded by farm land.

Paciolo was born into a lower middle-class family. His father was named Bartolomeo. The name of his mother is not known. Paciolo had at least two brothers, one who was much older and had sons Paciolo's age.

Since the family was relatively poor, Paciolo did not have a private tutor but went to religious schools. The major religious training in Borgo San Sepolcro was handled by the Franciscan Order. The education provided by the Franciscan friars was quite rigorous. As a youngster, Paciolo studied grammar, rhetoric (the drawing of documents and letter writing), and dialectic (logic). In addition, he had excellent training in

[2] Much of the information for our discussion of Paciolo's life came from the work by R. Emmett Taylor, NO ROYAL ROAD: LUCA PACIOLI AND HIS TIMES, Chapel Hill, The University of North Carolina Press, 1942.

religious matters, studying both the Bible and the teachings of St. Francis of Assisi.

As Paciolo matured he studied arithmetic, geometry, astronomy and music in addition to the classical literature available at the time, which included works by Dante, Cicero, Quintalian, Isidore of Seville, and Boethius. Paciolo was an eager student. Evidence of his scholarly inclinations was apparent to his teachers.

At the age of 16, boys were considered grown and ready for the responsibilities of adulthood. Paciolo was apprenticed to the family of Folco de Belfolci, a prominent businessman and a member of one of the artisan guilds. In the guilds, an apprentice moved in with a master workman and lived with him during the three to eleven years of his apprenticeship. Initially, the parents of the boy would pay a certain fee to the master workman for the training, but eventually the boy became self-supporting.

It was difficult for a young man to continue his education beyond the age of 16, unless he was born into wealth or nobility. Books were not readily available for self study, and studying at a university was considered a luxury. Paciolo was intent upon continuing his education and quit his apprenticeship in the guild in order to study with Piero della Francesca. Francesca was working in Borgo San Sepolcro during the 1460's.

It was customary in those times for artists of high reputation to have a number of young men studying under them. Although Francesca was primarily an artist, he was also a mathematician. He was interested in studying proportion and this interest was to influence Paciolo throughout his life. When he was 63 years old, Paciolo remarked in a lecture in Venice, "Of all arduous and difficult things . . . the most difficult is proportion."

Paciolo was greatly influenced by Francesca. During the time that Paciolo was studying with him, they made frequent trips to the town of Urbino, approximately forty miles away. The Duke of Urbino, Federigo, had one of the finest libraries in the world, and Paciolo was given free access to it. Federigo's fine library cost him 30,000 gold ducats, a small fortune. All of the books were bound in scarlet and silver and were written with a pen. It was said that they were so superlative that "had there been one printed volume, it would have been shamed in such company." This library was compared favorably with that of the papacy and with the University of Oxford, which were supposed to be the leading libraries of the time. Obviously, the Duke's library was not open to the general public, and it was with considerable pride and humility that Paciolo studied there.

Paciolo became close friends with the Duke of Urbino as well as the Duke's only son, Prince Guidobaldo. Guidobaldo was born in 1472 and studied with Paciolo on several occasions during the latter's frequent trips through Urbino. Paciolo dedicated his SUMMA to ". . . the most illustrious Prince Guidobaldo, Duke of Urbino . . . most learned in Greek and Latin letters, and a very keen student of the disciplines of mathematics." This dedication is a reflection of Paciolo's fondness for the Urbino family, and probably reflects his great appreciation for the opportunities provided him by Guidobaldo's father, Federigo. It is Guidobaldo who is standing beside Paciolo in the painting reproduced in this book.

By 1464, Francesca had developed great admiration for Paciolo and brought him to the attention of the great architect and author, Leon Battista Alberti. Alberti took Paciolo with him to Venice. While there, Paciolo not only studied, but acted as a house tutor for the three sons of a wealthy merchant, Ser Antonio de Rompiasi. Paciolo lived with the Rompiasi family and became so fond of his students that he dedicated his first manuscript, which was on the subject of mathematics, to them.

It was in the house of the merchant Rompiasi that Paciolo first taught arithmetic and bookkeeping. These subjects were felt necessary in order that the boys become good merchants. It is not known when Paciolo became familiar with the fundamentals of double-entry bookkeeping. Quite likely he had studied it in Borgo San Sepolcro with the master guildsman, Belfolci. However, since Paciolo undoubtedly taught the Rompiasi boys the Venetian method, he must have done some studying while he was in Venice. The treatise on bookkeeping, published in the SUMMA in 1494, arose out of this necessity to teach the double-entry process. It is doubtful that Paciolo ever worked as a bookkeeper.

While Paciolo was teaching the Rompiasi boys, he frequently travelled to Padua where he visited the University of Padua. This was the first contact that Paciolo had with the University. He was unable to break away from university life for the remainder of his career.

After the six year period with the Rompiasi family, Paciolo went to Tuscany to work with Alberti. Paciolo was still a student, spending most of his time studying under Alberti. Although Alberti was a successful architect, he is better known for his written works. He wrote 17 books, covering such subjects as architecture, painting, rules for measuring heights, prose and verse, a book about his family, and another containing a Latin comedy. It is no surprise that after spending many years with Francesca and Alberti, Paciolo was an extremely well educated individual. These two men were scholars of a high order. It is said that Alberti epitomized the thought of the early high Renaissance, just as Leonardo da Vinci incarnated the later high Renaissance.

After working in Tuscany, Paciolo accompanied Alberti to Rome. Alberti always was active in the church and a good friend of various Popes. Paciolo met Paul II through Alberti. Before coming to Rome in 1471, however, Paciolo led the life of the gay young blade in Venice. Although religious, he had not seriously contemplated taking the cloth until after meeting Alberti.

Alberti had exerted a great influence on Paciolo, encouraging him to write in the native tongue and to teach. Soon after Alberti's death in 1472, Paciolo decided to devote his life to those two endeavors. Since his youth, he had been close to the Franciscans. In addition, the current Pope was a Franciscan, and the Franciscans had a reputation for teaching. It therefore seemed desirable for Paciolo to join the Order himself.

It is apparent that this period of time, roughly the mid-1470's, witnessed the maturity of the young Paciolo. Paciolo was now about 30 years old and ready to take his first university teaching job and begin writing in earnest. The contributions made by Paciolo in the next 30 years rank him among the great of the Italian Renaissance.

The Mature Scholar

Although Paciolo was to continue studying for the rest of his life, he had reached the point at which he felt prepared to teach others. The first of his many teaching positions at universities was at Perugia, starting in 1475. It is quite possible that Paciolo got this teaching job through the influence of Pope Sixtus. Paciolo had come to know the Pope through Alberti when they were living in Rome. Prior to becoming Pope and taking the name of Sixtus IV, Francesco della Rovere had taught at the University of Perugia.

While at this University, Paciolo lectured on mathematics. At that time, mathematics was new to the university curriculum. Paciolo was the first university professor to fill a chair in mathematics. Paciolo stressed that theory was important but was of almost no value unless it could be put to practical use. He constantly lectured on this theme. In order to bring mathematics down to earth, Paciolo frequently used examples from his own personal experiences and applications from such fields as architecture and art.

During this period, the European universities did not require students to attend lectures, and many students would wander from one lecture to another, depending on their whims and the reputations of the professors. The relationship between students and competent professors was usually very close. Paciolo was well liked by his students because of his scholarly background and his ability to lecture. As his students graduated, Paciolo's reputation flourished throughout Italy.

Paciolo left Perugia in about 1480 to travel and study at the various universities in Italy. When he returned to Perugia in 1486, he had acquired the title of Magister or Master. This was the prevailing title in the faculties of the universities and considered the equivalent of the doctorate.

Paciolo stayed at Perugia for two years, leaving in 1488 to return to Rome. During this second term at the University of Perugia, Paciolo did considerable work on his SUMMA. He had started sometime around 1470, but a major portion of it was written between 1486 and 1488.

Upon his arrival in Rome, Paciolo taught mathematics at the university there until 1490. Sometime during the early 1490's he also taught at the University of Naples. It was about this time that Paciolo got in trouble with the Franciscan Order. Paciolo enjoyed teaching in universities and working on his books. However, the Franciscan brothers felt that he should teach in the secular schools. The Franciscan Order wrote several letters to Paciolo in 1491, indicating that the Order would use severe measures if he did not teach in the religious schools. Another document threatened him with excommunication and privation of office if he did not return to Padua in eight days. Apparently Paciolo was able to placate the Order because he continued to write and teach outside of the secular schools. It is also possible that he had his friend, Pope Innocent VIII, intercede in his behalf.

Immediately prior to 1494, Paciolo spent some time in Urbino working on his SUMMA and preparing it for publication. While there, he renewed his friendship with the Duke of Urbino, Guidobaldo. The Duke encouraged and assisted Paciolo in completing this project. The publication of the SUMMA brought considerable fame to Paciolo. It was the publication of the SUMMA that led directly to the friendship between Paciolo and Leonardo da Vinci.

Leonardo da Vinci was working in the court of Milan in the early 1490's. When he saw the SUMMA, he asked that Paciolo be brought to the court of Milan to teach mathematics. Paciolo arrived in 1496 to teach in the Court. While there he taught arithmetic, geometry, and military tactics at the University of Milan as well as in the Court. Paciolo and da Vinci became close friends, for they had common interests and they complemented each other in their skills. The fact that da Vinci was seven years younger than Paciolo did not affect this friendship. During these three years, 1496 to 1499, two classics were created by these two men: Leonardo da Vinci painted "The Last Supper," and Paciolo wrote his second major book, DE DIVINA PROPORTIONE.

Although da Vinci was well known during his lifetime, he did not achieve real fame until years after his death. On the other hand, Paciolo won fame early in his career and, because of his education and reputation, could go anywhere and meet anyone.

In 1499, both da Vinci and Paciolo left Milan and went to Florence. Paciolo accepted a teaching position at the University of Florence and taught there until 1506, with the exception of two years spent teaching at the University of Bologna in 1501 and 1502

While in Florence, Paciolo wrote a book on games entitled, SCHIFA-NOIA, which translates literally, "begone dull care." This was a book about games and included chess problems, magic squares and card games.

When Paciolo left the University of Florence in 1506, he went to the University of Pisa where he taught Euclidian geometry. His dissatisfaction with the current materials available for teaching led him to prepare a new translation of Euclid's geometry into Italian.

It was in the first decade of the 16th century that Paciolo reached the apex of his fame. Whenever he lectured in Venice, Florence, and Pisa, he packed the lecture rooms with some of the most famous people of the time.

Just prior to 1510, Paciolo was named the head of the monastery in Borgo San Sepolcro. However, he continued to come and go as he pleased and took a teaching position at the University of Perugia in 1510. Much to the despair of his Franciscan brothers, Paciolo spent very little time administering his responsibilities at the monastery at Borgo San Sepolcro. In fact, the second in charge at the San Sepolcro monastery questioned Paciolo's leadership, which again placed him in disfavor in the Franciscan Order.

In 1508, Pope Julius II issued a special papal bull which gave Paciolo the right to own personal property. This rather unusual privilege did not do much to endear Paciolo to his Franciscan brothers. However, there is no specific evidence that Paciolo was able to accumulate any significant amount of personal wealth.

By 1514, Paciolo had returned to teaching. He was then about 69 years old. Pope Leo X had decided to make the faculty of the University of Rome second to none. He brought distinguished professors from all over western Europe, and one of these was Paciolo. Paciolo was on the faculty roll of the University of Rome in the year 1514, and this is the last we know of him. It is possible that he died the following year, or that he resigned to spend his declining years in a monastery or with friends.

Paciolo stipulated in his will, prepared in 1511, that he be buried in Borgo San Sepolcro and that a tomb be erected in his memory. Apparently this request was never carried out, for there is no such tomb in this town or in its Franciscan monastery. It is quite likely that Paciolo died in Rome or some town other than San Sepolcro, such as Florence. If such was the case, it would have been extremely doubtful that his body would have been transported to San Sepolcro for burial.

Paciolo had led a rich life and had achieved deserved fame during his lifetime. His many written works, which were so widely used, represented a major contribution to his times. Translating theory into practice and doing it in a manner which the common people could understand, made Paciolo unique among his peers.

Taylor, in his book on Paciolo's life, has an excellent comment on this era of civilization and Paciolo's role in it.

> Pacioli lived through the "Golden Age of the Renaissance," a period which marked the apogee of what we call the finer things of life. It challenges the imagination to visualize an age when so many great people lived. We must envy him on a walk when, in the course of a short distance, he was able to encounter many men whose names five hundred years later are familiar to the ears of every intelligent person. We can see him chatting with the great and noble prince, the Grand Man of Urbino; with his old master Piero, who was shaping the art of the future; with the aristocratic and aggressive Alberti, who could play the organ, or jump over a horse, or build a temple; with the quiet and retiring Leonardo of the flowing beard who could tinker with a flying machine or paint a "Mona Lisa," in short, with people in all walks of life who were eager to improve their present and to leave something of substance to the future. We must envy him his breadth of interest. Now he is writing a book; now he is lecturing at the university; now he is advising military men how to lay siege to a city; now he is struggling along a mountain road to an inaccessible chapel to chat with some artist about the art of perspective; now he is discussing theology with the prelates; now he drops into a humble shop and advises the merchant how to keep his books; now he pauses in the square to watch a football game or a horse race.

Unfortunately, the closest that we can get to this great man is to become familiar with the written works which he created during his lifetime.

SECTION II

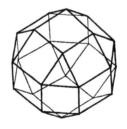

The Translation of the
Bookkeeping Treatise

CONTENTS

Paciolo's Treatise on Bookkeeping

PARTICULARIS DE COMPUTIS ET SCRIPTURIS

23

Chapter 1

Those Things Necessary to the Successful Businessman.
Methods of Properly Keeping a Ledger and Journal in
Venice and Elsewhere.

In addition to the subjects already dealt with in this book, I have prepared this greatly needed special treatise so that the respectful subjects of the Duke of Urbino may have all the rules that successful businessmen require.[1] The present treatise is included for this reason only: It will serve all the needs of the subjects regarding accounts and recording. Therefore, I intend to give sufficient rules to enable businessmen to keep all their accounts and books in an orderly fashion.

There are three things necessary to one who wishes to operate a business successfully. The most important is cash, or some equivalent economic power. Without this, operating a business would be extremely difficult. As the saying goes, "One thing is necessary: substance." Many people throughout Italy have carried on a substantial business with little more than good faith and, because of their ability to obtain credit, have attained wealth. In the great republics, oaths were taken "on the word of a good businessman," indicating the great confidence in their integrity. This is not unusual because truly everyone is saved by faith, without which it is impossible to please God.

The second thing necessary in business is to be a good accountant and a ready mathematician. The regular rules and canons necessary to each transaction are given so that any careful reader can understand it and become proficient. The reader should understand mathematics (as given in previous sections of the book), for that which follows depends on such an understanding.

---

[1] It should be remembered that Paciolo dedicated the entire SUMMA to Guidobaldo, Duke of Urbino. In several places in the SUMMA, Paciolo again mentions the Duke. This treatise on bookkeeping is no exception.

The third and last thing necessary is that all the businessman's affairs be arranged in a systematic way so that he may get their particulars at a glance. The debit and credit method should be used, since business is best described in this way. This is essential to businessmen, for without systematic recording, their minds would always be so tired and troubled that it would be impossible for them to conduct business. Therefore, I have arranged this treatise in step-by-step fashion, presenting the method for recording all sorts of entries. Although I cannot write all that ought to be written on the subject, a careful reader will be able to apply the methods illustrated to his special situation.

The system employed in Venice will be adopted here, for it is certainly recommended above all others. In grasping it, the businessman will be able to understand any other system. This work is divided into two principal parts: The Inventory and the Disposition. I shall discuss the former first and then the latter, following the order set forth in the table of contents.

Let him who wants to know how to keep an orderly Ledger and its Journal pay strict attention. So that the reader may fully understand the procedure, the case of one who is just starting in business will be used. How to keep accounts and books will be illustrated in order that each thing can easily be found in its proper place. If each thing is not in its right place, great trouble and confusion would arise. As the saying goes, "Where there is no order, there is chaos."

As mentioned above, a perfect model will be given to every businessman and will be divided into two principal parts. These will be made quite clear separately so that fruitful results may be obtained from them.

Chapter 2

The First Part of This Treatise: The Inventory—What It Is and How It Should Be Taken by Businessmen.

First, I assume that each businessman is working toward an end, and that he makes use of every effort to satisfy this end. The end or objective of every businessman is to make a lawful and satisfactory profit, so that he may remain in business. Therefore, businessmen should commence their affairs with the name of God at the beginning of every book, always bearing His holy name in mind.

The businessman must then prepare his Inventory in the following way: First of all, he must write on a sheet of paper or in a separate book all his worldly belongings, that is, his personal property or real estate. He should always begin with the things that are more valuable and easier to lose. These consist of such things as ready cash, jewels, and silver. Real estate, such as houses, land, lakes, meadows, and ponds cannot be as easily mislaid as personal property. He must then record all other things in proper order in the Inventory. However, the day, the year, the place and his name must always be recorded first. The entire inventory must be completed on the same day, otherwise there will be future difficulty in managing the business.

I will now give you an example of how the inventory should be taken.

Chapter 3

An Example of an Inventory with All Its Formalities.

In the Name of God
November 8, 1493
Venice

The following is the Inventory of myself of Venice, Street of the Holy Apostles.

I have written down systematically, or have had written by Mr. Bookkeeper,[2] all my personal and real property, as well as that which is owed me and that which I owe on this day.

First Item

I have cash composed of both gold and coin of so many *ducats*, of which so many are gold Venetians, so many gold Hungarians, and so many Papal, Siennese and Florentine large *florins*. The remainder consists of various kinds of silver and copper coins, that is *troni, marcelli,* and *carlini* of the Pope and of the royalty, Florentine *grossi*, and Milanese *testoni*.

Second Item

I have so many pieces of set and unset jewels among which are many rubies set in flat-surfaced settings and gold rings weighing so many

---

[2] Paciolo uses personal pronouns such as "Mr. So-and-So" throughout. We have changed these abstract references to more familiar terms, such as "Mr. Bookkeeper" and "Mr. Businessman."

ounces, carats, or grains per piece or in total, (you may express this in your own way). There are so many sapphires set for women, and so many unset rubies weighing so much. The remainder consists of uncut diamonds weighing in total so many points. Here you may describe the type and weight as you desire.

Third Item

I have clothes of so many kinds. You may describe their condition, colors, linings, and styles.

Fourth Item

I have various kinds of silverware such as cups, basins, coppers, spoons, and pegs. Carefully describe and weigh each kind separately. Keep an account of the pieces, their weights and alloys, and whether they are Venetian, Ragusan, etc., and the stamp or mark that may be on them.

Fifth Item

I have so much cloth and linen, such as bedsheets, tablecloths, shirts, and handkerchiefs. Of the bedsheets, some are three-piece sheets, others two-and-one-half. There is Paduan linen[3] and other kinds, new or used and of so many arm-lengths. There are so many new or used shirts, tablecloths of so many threads and so large, and so many small handkerchiefs. Describe these items in your own way.

Sixth Item

I have so many new or used featherbeds, pillows, and pillow-cases, weighing so many pounds separately or in total, having my mark or some other.

---

[3] It was the custom in the 15th century in Italy to mention any special desirable characteristics of goods, such as geographical origin. Such a custom persists today.

Seventh Item

I have goods of various kinds at home or in warehouses. There are so many marked cases of *mechini* ginger weighing so many pounds. Describe each kind of such goods in detail by their marks. Give in the most accurate manner their weights, numbers, and measurements.

Eighth Item

I have so many cases of *bellidi* ginger and so many sacks of pepper of long or round type. There are also so many bundles of cinnamon, weighing so much; so many cases of cloves, with casks or without, weighing so much; so many cases of brazilwood, weighing so much; and so many pieces of red or white sandalwood, weighing so much. Continue entering one item after another in this way in proper order.

Ninth Item

I have skins for coverings, that is, so many white kid of such kinds as Albertoni Pugliesi or Marchiani, so many raw or tanned Marchiani fox skins, and so many raw or tanned chamois skins.

Tenth Item

I have very fine Armenti seal skins and various sable skins of so many of each kind.

Carefully and truthfully describe each item in its turn. Let truth always be your guide. Carefully distinguish the items by numbers, weight, or measurement, because it is customary everywhere to conduct business in these three ways. Certain things are classed by thousands, others by hundreds, others by pounds, others by ounces, others by number, others by unit (as with leather goods of skins), others by piece (as with jewels and fine pearls). Record each of them individually. These examples will guide you in determining other cases.

30

Eleventh Item

I have real estate of a house of so many stories, so many rooms, a court-yard, wells, gardens, and located on the street of the Holy Apostles over the canal, adjoining various specified places. Record the names of the adjoining properties, referring to the oldest and most reliable deeds available. If you have houses in other localities, enter them in a similar way.

Twelfth Item

I have so many acres under cultivation, measuring so many *tavole*, *canne, partiche*, or *bevolche*. Enter their size and description according to the usage in the country in which you or the lands are situated. Record their location near a certain town or somewhere else, and the persons' land which they border. Give the boundary lines, referring to deeds of tax receipts of the municipality to which you pay taxes on the lands. Name the tenant who cultivates the land and the yearly income of so many bushels and so much money. Continue entering thus all your possessions, such as cattle.

Thirteenth Item

I have so many *ducats* on deposit with the Camera de l'Impresti and other Venetian banks, so many in the district of Canareggio, or part in one district and part in another. Give the names under which the *ducats* have been deposited, mentioning the book of the bank and the page number where your amount is stated. Give the name of the clerk who keeps the book so that you will be able to withdraw your money readily when you wish, because in such banks many accounts must be kept to serve the multitude that go to them. Carefully note the dates of their correspondence, so that you know the amount due you and what percentage they are answerable for.

Fourteenth Item

I have so many debtors. One is Mr. Buyer, who owes me so many *ducats*. Name the debtors by their full names, where they live, how much they owe, and why. Mention whether there are written papers or notarial instruments between you. Indicate that you have so many *ducats* of good money to collect, which is the money due from reliable people. Otherwise, call their money bad.

Fifteenth Item

I have debts amounting to so many *ducats*. I owe so many to Mr. Seller. Give the names of your creditors in this way one by one. State whether everything is clear between you and if there are any written papers or instruments. Mention the persons present when the debt was incurred, how it was incurred, and the time and the place; all these particulars may be necessary for any case in or out of court.

Chapter 4

Warnings and Helpful Advice to the
Successful Businessman.

Carefully record all personal property and real estate, item by item, (even if there were ten thousand), entering their condition and nature, and whether deposited or loaned. Every item must be systematically recorded in the Inventory with all countermarks, full names, and in as much detail as possible. Because of the vast number of things that might occur, transactions can never be too clear to a businessman. Right is the proverb which says, "More skills are required to make a successful businessman than are required to make a good lawyer."

Who can count all the things that befall the businessman—on land and sea, in times of peace and plenty and war and famine, in times of health and pestilence? During these changing times, he must know what to do in the market and at fairs, which are held here and there. Because of this, a businessman rightly resembles a rooster which is the most alert animal that exists, for among other things, it keeps night vigils in winter and summer, never resting. It is said that the nightingale sings throughout the night, but this is true in the summer during hot weather and not during winters, as experience shows.

It is said that a businessman's head has a hundred eyes, yet these are not enough for all he has to say or to do. These things are said by those who know, such as the Venetians, Florentines, Genoese, Neopolitans, Milanese, Anconians, Brescians, Bergamenes, Aquileians, Sienese, Lucchesi, Perugians, Urbinians, Forosempronians, Cagliesi, Ugubrians, Castellani, Borghesi, Fulignati, Pisans, Bolognese, Ferrarese, Mantuans, Veronese, Vigentians, Paduans, Trani, Lecce, Bari, and Betonti which represent the leading commercial cities of Italy. The cities of Venice and Florence are the greatest of them, adopting rules and regulations that respond to any need. As the municipal laws correctly say, "The law helps those that are awake, not those that sleep."

In the divine offices of the Holy Church, they sing that God promised a crown to the watchful. This was Virgil's instruction to Dante, as to his own son in Canto 24 of the Inferno, where he exhorts him to labor, as the only means in which one can attain the mount of Virtue: "Alas my son, it is necessary that you quit your laziness, for one does not achieve success by lying on feathers or under quilts. He who wastes his life in this way leaves on this earth a trace similar to that left by smoke in the air or by foam on the water." Another Italian poet admonishes us in the same way saying, "Work should not appear strange to you, for Mars never granted victory to those that spent their time resting." It is also very good to quote the sage telling the lazy man to take the ant as an example. Paul the Apostle says that no one is worthy of the crown except he who valiantly fights for it.

I have added these reminders for your own good, so that you will give your affairs daily attention. Record everything that you require day by day, in the manner stated in the following chapters. But above all keep God before your eyes, never forgetting to attend to religious meditation every morning, as the following holy verse says: "Time is not wasted by religious meditation any more than wealth is lost by charity." And to this our Savior exhorts us in St. Matthew, when he says: ". . . seek ye first the kingdom of God, and his righteousness; and all these things shall be added unto you."

I hope this will be sufficient instruction for the Inventory, and for doing similar things well.

34

Chapter 5

The Second Part of This Treatise: Disposition—What Is to be Understood by It, What It Consists of in Business, and the Three Principal Books of Businessmen.

Now comes the second part of this treatise, which is called Disposition. In order to make it clear to you, I must deal with it at more length than the first part. I will divide it into two parts: One shall deal with your commerce in general, and the other your store in particular.

First, I shall speak of your commerce in general and the handling of its requirements.

Immediately after taking the Inventory, three books are required for your help and convenience: One is called the Memorandum, the second the Journal, and the third the Ledger. Many use only the Journal and the Ledger because of the smallness of their businesses. I shall speak first of the Memorandum and subsequently of the other two, their appearance, and how they should be kept. I shall first describe the Memorandum.

Chapter 6

The First Book, Called the Memorandum, Scrap Book, or Household Expense Book. What Is to be Understood by It, How Entries Should be Made in It, and by Whom.

The Memorandum, or as it is sometimes called, Scrap Book or Household Expense Book, is a book in which the businessman records all his transactions, large and small, in chronological order regardless of their size. He will record in detail in this book everything bought or sold, omitting nothing, clearly mentioning the who, what, when, and where of the transaction, such as previously described in connection with the Inventory. Many businessmen customarily record their Inventory in this book. However, it is not wise to enter personal and real property here since it passes through many hands and before many eyes.

The Memorandum is needed because of the volume of business done. Entries should be made in it by the owner, or in the absence of the owner, by his agents, assistants, or his women (if they know how). A big businessman never keeps his assistants idle.

Businessmen and their assistants are frequently at fairs and markets. Only the women or other assistants remain at home, and they can barely write.[4] However, in order not to refuse customers, they must buy, sell, or collect according to the orders left by the owner. As best they can, they must enter every transaction in the Memorandum, describing it in terms of the money and weights they know, noting the various types of monies collected or given in exchange. It is not necessary to standardize monies in this book, although it is required in the Journal and the Ledger.

[4] Italian women during the 15th century rarely received formal education. They played a secondary role in society, scarcely breaking away from household duties. As a reflection of this, Paciolo's mother's name is never mentioned, nor is it known whether he had a sister.

The bookkeeper will put everything in order, and then record the transactions in the Journal. When the owner returns he will see all of the transactions and record them over again if he thinks it necessary. Therefore, for those who do a substantial business, it would be useless trouble to record orderly and in diligently kept authentic books all transactions as they take place.

When in the course of business, the Memorandum or other book is filled up or has served a certain period of time, a mark must be made on its cover and the cover of all other books. When any book has been used entirely, you must take another. Many businessmen in different localities are accustomed to balancing all of their books annually even though they have not been filled.

To preserve order, a mark different from that placed on the first book must be recorded on the second, so that your transactions can be promptly traced at any time. The date is required again for this reason. Among the Christians it is the good custom to initially mark their books with that glorious sign from which all enemies of the spiritual flee, and before which all the infernal pack justly tremble: The Sign of the Holy Cross, by which, in your early years, you commenced to learn the alphabet. Mark the books that follow in alphabetical order, an *A* for the second, *B* for the third, and so on, identifying the first set of books with crosses, that is, Memorandum ✠, Journal ✠, and Ledger ✠ The second set of books would be marked Memorandum *A*, Journal *A* and so on.

All these books must have their pages numbered for the many reasons known to the businessman. However, many say that this is not necessary in the Journal and Memorandum, because transactions are entered chronologically in such a way that they are easy to find. This is correct if daily transactions do not cover more than one page; however, many of the bigger merchants fill not one but several pages in one day. If someone wished to defraud, he could tear a page out and this fraud could not be discovered by reference to dates, because the days would follow chronologically and the page would not be missed. For this and other reasons, therefore, it is always good practice to number and sign each page of all business books kept in the house or in the store.

Chapter 7

The Manner in Which All Business Books Are to be Authenticated, Why, and by Whom.

In the several countries where I have found it necessary to take business books, it is the good custom to present them to a certain Commerce Officer (such as the Consuls in the employ of the City of Perosa). He should be told that these are the books in which you intend to record, or have someone else record, all your transactions. He should also know in what kind of monies and weights the transactions will be entered, whether in units of *lire* and *picioli*, *lire* and *grossi*, *ducats* and *lire*, *florins* and *lire*, or in ounces, *tari*, *denari*, or grains. The good businessman must always put these things down on the first page of his book. When someone other than the one stated at the beginning of the book is to make the entries, it is best to inform the pertinent officer.

All this will be entered in the register of the officer by the clerk, saying that on a certain day you presented certain business books marked with a given mark; one book called the Memorandum, the other the Journal, and so on, of which the first has so many pages, the other so many. These books would be kept by you or by your bookkeeper, except that in the one called the Memorandum, Scrap Book, or Household Expense Book, all members of your family or household might enter transactions.

In the name of his officer, the clerk will write all this on the first page of your books and will attest to its truth. He will then attach the seal of the pertinent officer which will make them authentic for any situation in which their presentation might be required. This custom should be fully commended, as should the places where it is observed.

Unfortunately, there are many who keep their books in duplicate, showing one to the buyer and the other to the seller. What is worse, they swear and perjure themselves upon them. How wrongly they act!

However, if they must present their books to an officer they cannot so easily lie and defraud.

These books, carefully marked and authenticated, are kept at home. Here, in the name of God, you will record your transactions. Enter in your Journal in an orderly way all the items in the Inventory, in the way that you will learn later. First, however, you must understand how entries should be made in the Memorandum.

Chapter 8

How Entries Are to be Made in the Memorandum,
With Examples.

Anyone in your family or household can make entries in the Memorandum, Scrap Book or Household Expense Book. Consequently, one cannot fully state how the entries should be made, because some persons might or might not understand. The common custom is this: For example, assume that you have purchased so many pieces of cloth, say twenty white Bresciani for twelve *ducats* apiece. This transaction can be recorded as follows:

> On this day, we have (or I have) bought from Filippo de Ruffoni of Brescia, twenty pieces of white Bresciani cloth. They are stored in Stefano Tagliapietra's vault and are of so many arm lengths apiece, as agreed upon. They cost twelve *ducats* each and are marked with a certain number. Mention if the cloth is made of triple warp-cord, four to five arm lengths square, wide or narrow, fine or medium, whether Bergamene, Vicenzan, Veronese, Paduan, Florentine, or Mantuan. State whether the transaction was made entirely for cash, or part only for cash and part on time. State when the balance is due or whether payment was partly for cash and the remainder in goods.

If payment is to be made in goods, you must specify the items given in exchange; their number, weight, and measurement, and the price per bushel, or pound, etc. If the transaction were on an account basis, state the time when payment should be made (e.g. on the return of ships, such as Barutto's ships or Flander's ships, or at the end of fairs or other festivities, such as harvest day or next Easter, Christmas, Resurrection Day or Carnival Day). No point should be omitted in the Memorandum. If it were possible, everything that was said during the transaction would be noted. As mentioned previously, transactions can never be too clear to a businessman.

Chapter 9

*The Nine Ways in Which It Is Customary for Businessmen
to Buy. The Goods Which It Is More or Less Necessary
to Buy on Time.*

Since we are speaking of buying, note that you may commonly make
purchases in nine ways: First, in cash; second, on time; third, by the
exchange of goods; fourth, by draft; fifth, partly in cash and partly on
time; sixth, partly in cash and partly by goods; seventh, partly by
goods and partly on time; eighth, partly by draft and partly on time;
ninth, partly by draft and partly in goods. It is customary to make purchases in these nine ways.[5] If you buy in some other way, enter precisely what you have done in the Memorandum or have someone else
enter it.

It is customary to buy on time when you buy wheat or oats, wines,
salt, leather from butchers, and fats. In these cases, the seller promises
to give the buyer the wheat he will produce during that season. Similarly, the butcher will promise you all the hearts, skins, fat, etc., which
he will obtain during that year at so much per pound for one thing and
so much for another, such as beef fat and mutton. Black and white mutton skins would be charged by the piece; oats and corn charged by
bushel or basket, depending on local custom which differs at Chiusi and
Perugia. State whether the wheat came from such places as our city San
Sepolcro, or Mercattello, Sant'Angelo, Citta di Castello, or Forli, etc.

Thus, whether entering transactions in the Memorandum for yourself or others, mention everything in full, item by item. State things
simply, just as they happened. The skillful bookkeeper will transfer
chronologically these transactions from the Memorandum to the Journal. He will do this in four, five, or eight days, more or less, except it

---

[5] Paciolo omits a tenth, partly by cash and partly by draft. However, he mentions
this in Chapter 19.

is unnecessary for him to transfer all the detail to the Journal, since references could later be made from one book to the other. Those that have kept three books, (Memorandum, Journal and Ledger), must never enter anything in the Journal if it has not first been entered in the Memorandum.

This should be sufficient regarding the arrangement of the Memorandum, whether it is kept for you or for others. Note that there are as many ways to sell as to buy. Knowing the ways of buying, you will understand how to sell. Therefore, I need not explain ways of selling.

Chapter 10

The Second Important Business Book Called the Journal.
What It Is and How It Must be Kept in an Orderly Way.

The second common business book is called the Journal, which must bear the same mark that is on the Memorandum and have its pages marked as specified for the Memorandum. Always place the date and day at the beginning of each page, and then enter consecutively all the items of your Inventory.

Since the Journal is your private book, you may state fully what you own in personal or real property, always referring to the pertinent inventory documents. These are usually kept in some chest, box, on a string, or in a pouch as is customary with letters and trifles. The different journal entries ought to be entered and arranged in a neat and systematic way, neither superfluously nor too briefly, as the following few examples will show.

First of all, though, you should note the necessity of two expressions necessary to keeping a Journal, which are used according to the custom of the great city of Venice.

Chapter 11

The Two Expressions Used in the Journal, Especially in
Venice: One Called Per, *and the other* A, *and*
What Is to be Understood by Them.

There are two unique expressions used in the Journal: One is called
Per and the other *A*, each having a meaning of its own.

Per always indicates a debit, one or more as the case may be.

A denotes a credit, one or more as the case may be.

An ordinary item is never entered in the Journal (which will be later
posted to the Ledger) unless it contains the two expressions. The expression *Per* is put at the beginning of each entry, because the debit
must always be described first; and then, immediately after, *A* and the
credit. One is separated from the other by two small slanting parallel
lines "//," as you will note in the example given in Chapter 12.[6]

---

[6] Subsequent authors on bookkeeping used the same construction for journal entries as did Paciolo. However, they changed *Per* to "from" and *A* to "to." As can
be seen in the next chapter, we have forsaken both in preference to common debit
and credit usage. Paciolo's entries appear as in this example: *Per* Cash / / *A* Capital.

Chapter 12

*How to Enter and Arrange Items in the Journal by Means
of Debit and Credit Entries, With Many Examples. The Two
Other Expressions Used in the Ledger, the One Called Cash and
the Other Capital, and What is to be Understood by Them.*

In the name of God enter in the Journal the first item of your Inventory,
which is the quantity of money that you possess. In order to know how
to enter this Inventory in the Journal and Ledger, you must make use
of two other terms; one is called Cash, and the other Capital. Cash
means the money on hand. Capital means the entire amount of what
you now possess.

At the beginning of all business Journals and Ledgers, Capital must
always be entered as a credit and Cash always as a debit. In the management of any type of business, Cash may never have a credit balance,
but only debit (unless it balances). If, in balancing your book, you find
that Cash has a credit balance, an error in the book is indicated. Cash
must always be entered in the Journal in the following way:

Examples for Making Journal Entries.

8th day of November, MCCCCLXXXXIII, in Venice.

First

1   debit line[7]

2

Debit Cash, credit Capital of myself, Mr. Businessman. At present I have cash in a certain place, consisting
of gold, coin, silver, and copper of various coinage as
shown on the first sheet of the Inventory, in total so
many gold *ducats* and so many *ducats* in coin. In our
Venetian money all is valued in gold, that is, 24 *grossi*
for each *ducat* and 32 *picioli* for each *grosso*, and so
many gold *lire*.

credit line

Value:

L. . *(lire)* S. . *(soldi)* G. . *(grossi)* P. . *(picioli)*

[7] Paciolo suggests that when the debit entry is posted to the Ledger, a vertical
line be drawn to the left of the journal entry. When the credit is posted, a "credit

45

Record the second item as follows:

Second   Debit Jewels of various kinds, credit Capital for so many mounted rubies weighing so much, so many unset sapphires, rubies, and diamonds, etc., as they appear in the above Inventory. Record these values at current prices, the rubies worth so much, etc., and continue stating at current prices each kind which in total amount to so many *ducats*.
Value:

$$L. . . , S. . . , G. . . , P. . .$$

If you have already named the day, the debit and the credit, and if no other item is entered in between, for brevity you may record: "On this same day, debit ditto, credit ditto."

Third   Debit Silverware, credit Capital for the several kinds of silver in my possession at present: So many basins, so many coppers, so many cups, so many pegs, and so many spoons, weighing so much in total.
Value:

$$L. . . , S. . . , G. . . , P. . .$$

In making entries in the Journal, record all the pertinent details you described in the Inventory, giving each thing a customary price for your own personal knowledge. Make the prices high rather than low. If it seems to you that something is worth 20, put it down at 24, so that you will make a larger profit. You will enter everything in this way, one by one, with its respective weight, number, and value.

Fourth   Debit Woolen Clothes, credit Capital for so many clothes of certain styles and colors, lined, in new or used condition, etc., for myself, my wife, or my children. I give the total value in *ducats*, in accordance with the current price. For cloaks and all the other clothes, I enter so many of a certain color, etc.
Value:

$$L. . . , S. . . , G. . . , P. . .$$

---

posting line" be drawn to the right of the journal entry. The two numbers at the left of the debit posting line are the folio references giving respectively, the Ledger page number of the debit and credit entry. Paciolo describes this posting process in detail in Chapter 14.

| *Fifth* | Debit Linen, credit Capital for so many bedsheets, etc., recording the number and value for everything shown in the Inventory. |

Value:

$$L. \ldots, S. \ldots, G. \ldots, P. \ldots$$

| *Sixth* | Debit Featherbeds, credit Capital for so much in feathers. Put down their number, value, and the necessary detail shown in the Inventory. |

Value:

$$L. \ldots, S. \ldots, G. \ldots, P. \ldots$$

| *Seventh* | Debit *Mechini* Ginger, credit Capital for the number of cases and their current value in *ducats* as contained in the Inventory. |

Value:

$$L. \ldots, S. \ldots, G. \ldots, P. \ldots$$

Continue in this way to enter all the other items, making a separate entry for each different lot as was done for the ginger, giving the current prices of each, their number, markings, and weights as shown in the Inventory. Indicate the kind of money you want for each item. However, when summing the values only one kind of money should appear, since it would not be proper to total different kinds.

Close each journal entry by drawing a line from the end of the last word of the explanation of the entry to the figures obtained. You will do the same in the Memorandum, drawing a single diagonal line through each entry in this manner, "/," showing that the item has been entered in the Journal. Should you not wish to draw this line through the entry, mark through the first letter at the beginning of the entry, or the last letter at the end. In any event, use some sign by which you understand that the item has been transferred to the Journal.

Although you may use various expressions and signs, you must nevertheless attempt to use those common to other businessmen, so that you will not appear deficient in the usual business customs.

Chapter 13

*The Third and Last Principal Business Book Called the
Ledger. How It Is to be Kept Double With Its Index,
or Single Without.*

After all the transactions in the Journal have been entered in an orderly
manner, you must post them to the third book called the Ledger. The
Ledger usually contains twice as many pages as the Journal. It should
contain an Alphabet or Repertory, or as some call it, an Index (the
Florentines call it *Stratto*). Enter in the Index all debits and credits in
alphabetical order, together with the numbers of their respective pages:
Those names that begin with the letter *A*, on the page marked *A*, and
so on. It will be best to assign the marks to the pages of the Ledger that
correspond to those that appear on the Journal and Memorandum.

Having numbered the pages of the Ledger and placed the date at the
top at the right and left margin, enter Cash as a debit on the first page,
as it is in the Journal. Reserve the entire first page for Cash; do not
enter anything else as a debit or credit, because cash entries are more
numerous than all others. This is because money is almost continuously
being received or withdrawn, therefore, it needs much space. The Ledger must be ruled with as many lines as there are kinds of money which
you intend to enter. If you enter *lire, soldi, denari;* and *picioli,* draw
four lines. In front of the *lire* draw another line in order to record the
page number of the related debit and credit entries. In front of all these
lines draw two more wherein the dates may be entered for each entry.
As was seen in the other books, this will assist in finding the entries
quickly. This book shall also bear the Sign of the Cross.

Chapter 14

Posting Entries from the Journal into the Ledger, and Why
for Each Entry in the Journal There Are Two Made in the
Ledger. How Entries in the Journal Should be Cancelled.
The Two Ledger Page Numbers Which Are Placed
in the Margin of Each Entry.

Each of the entries made in the Journal must be posted twice in the Ledger, one to the debit and the other to the credit. In the Journal, the debit is indicated by *Per* and the credit by *A*. You must have an entry for each of them in the Ledger, the debit entry on the left side, and the credit on the right. In the debit posting, indicate the page number where the respective credit entry is to be found. Similarly, the credit entry must state where the related debit entry is to be found. All the items in the Ledger are cross referenced in this way, and you must never post a transaction to the debit without posting the related credit, nor must you ever make a credit entry without its respective amount being ready to be entered as a debit. The balancing of the Ledger depends on this.

The books cannot be closed unless the debits equal the credits. In other words, if all the debit entries were added on a separate sheet (even if there were ten thousand), and the credit entries were summed, the total of one should equal the total of the other. If it appears otherwise, some error has been made in the Ledger. This will be explained fully in Chapter 32, which deals with the trial balance. Since two postings are made in the Ledger for each entry in the Journal, draw two lines flanking the journal entry. If you post the debit first, draw a vertical line at the left of the journal entry. This shows that it has been debited in the Ledger. When the credit entry is posted, draw a vertical line to the right of the journal entry. It is possible to post the credit entry immediately or later, for the bookkeeper often is able to make two or three

49

entries on the same page, thus avoiding coming back to write on that same Ledger page later.

These two lines will appear as is shown in the margins by the first Cash entry in Chapter 12. One is called the debit posting line and the other the credit posting line.

In the left margin at the side of the journal entry, you must write down two numbers, one under the other. The top number indicates the page of the Ledger to which the debit was posted, the lower one denotes the pages of the Ledger to which the credit entry was posted. In the Cash entry in Chapter 12, it is shown $\frac{1}{2}$, without a line between the numbers. Some bookkeepers customarily place a line between $\frac{1}{2}$. This is not important, but it certainly looks better without the dividing line, for the figures do not appear broken or separated. The figure "1" means that Cash was debited on the first page of the Ledger. Capital was credited on the second page of the Ledger.

The closer the credit is posted to the debit, the nicer it will look. However, it really does not make any difference where the credit is posted. Because an entry of a different date is sometimes placed between the debit and credit entries in the Ledger, it may not look well. Difficulty may also be caused when searching for the related entries (as he who has tried knows). Since everything cannot be fully explained here, you must guide yourself with native ingenuity. However, always try in the Journal to place the credit following the debit on the same line or on the line immediately following; do not enter anything else in between. The same day that sees the origin of the debit also sees the credit. For this reason, place the one entry as near as possible to the other.

Chapter 15

*The Way in Which Cash and Capital Entries Should be
Posted in the Ledger. The Date Which Is Written at the
Top of the Page According to Ancient Custom. Changing
the Date. How to Arrange the Space on the Pages
for Small and Large Accounts in Accordance With the
Requirements of the Business.*

Now that you have been instructed in these things, the first entry of
Chapter 12 shall be posted to the Ledger, debiting Cash and crediting
Capital. But first, write down the year in the Ledger using Roman nu-
merals: MCCCCLXXXXIII. It is not customary to put the day at the
top of the Ledger as is done in the Journal. This is because one account
in the Ledger will cover several days, and therefore you cannot observe
chronological order for days by putting them at the top. The day is
recorded in the body of the entry. The reason for this will be explained
more fully in Chapter 16.

When the entry pertains to a different year from that shown at the
top of the page, record the year just before the entry. This happens only
when books are not balanced and transferred at the end of each year.
This is necessary only in the Ledger, as is shown below. Use the ancient
letters in making this entry, if only for the sake of more beauty (although it does not matter).

Therefore, post it this way:

Jesus . . . . . MCCCCLXXXXIII.
Debit Cash on November 8th, credit Capital for cash of different
kinds in gold and other coins, page 2.
L. . . , S. . . , G. . . , P. . . .

Having already given the description in the Journal, you need not
be lengthy in the Ledger. At the beginning of a page state everything

fully, but in subsequent entries on the same page just say, "On a certain day, debit Cash, page . . . , credit Capital, L. . . , S. . . , G. . . , P. . ."

After posting the entry, draw the "debit posting line" as explained in Chapter 12. Then enter Capital (on the credit side) as follows:

Jesus . . . . . *MCCCCLXXXXIII.*

Credit Capital, of my own, on November 8th, debit Cash for cash
of different kinds in gold and other coins, page 1.

L. . . , S. . . , G. . . , P. . . .

It is sufficient to be brief in making this entry. If other items are to be entered in the same account until the page is complete, it will be sufficient to use the word "ditto" when dates remain the same or when accounts do not change. I will give you an example at the end of this treatise.

Continue expressing yourself briefly in this manner, especially in those things which are private to you (that is, those things about which you do not have to give an account to anyone). However, for those things about which an account must be given to others, be more descriptive, even though you can always rely on the explanations found in the Journal.

After having done these things, the credit posting line may be inserted in the Journal. In the left margin, next to the entry, place the page numbers where the debit and credit entries are to be found, the debit above and the credit below. Immediately enter the debit and credit account in the Index, each under its own letter. Cash will be placed under the letter C as follows, "Cash, page 1." Place Capital also under C, "Capital of my own, page 2." In this way, continue entering in the Index all debit and credit accounts under their respective letters, in alphabetical order. When this is done, the accounts can easily be located in the Ledger.

Note that if the Ledger were lost for any reason, such as robbery, fire, or shipwreck, but either of the other two books remain (the Memorandum or the Journal), you would always be able to make up another Ledger containing the same entries on the same pages as was in the lost book. This is especially true if the two Ledger page numbers of the debit and credit entry have been posted in the Journal beside the journal entry. By using a little ingenuity, you will be able to reproduce your Ledger. This is sufficient instruction for the posting of this entry.

For the entry in the Journal which refers to Jewels, post it to the Ledger in its proper place, writing the date at the top of the page (providing the date has not already been written down for a previous entry). Sometimes, when the bookkeeper knows that the space is sufficient to contain two or three accounts, he will enter them on the same page. In this case the date would already appear. Consequently, these accounts will require smaller space than accounts which have a large number of entries. When many like transactions occur, the whole page is customarily used. As previously mentioned, this is the case with Cash and Capital.

Having found the proper place in the Ledger, post the debit entry on the left.

> Debit Jewels of many kinds on November 8th, credit Capital for so many pieces, weighing so much individually and in total; so many mounted rubies, so many sapphires, so many unset rubies, and so many uncut diamonds which I value by current prices at so many *ducats*, page 2.
>
> L. . . , S. . . , G. . . , P. . . .

Then draw the debit posting line in the Journal. Next go to Capital and post the credit entry in brief, entering it under the entry already posted to Capital:

> On the same day, credit Capital, debit Jewels of many kinds as they appear on page 3.
>
> L. . . , S. . . , G. . . , P. . . .

After this draw another line cancelling the credit side of the entry in the Journal. Place in the left margin the numbers of the two pages of the Ledger in which you have made these entries. If the debit entry were posted on page three, Capital will still appear on page two until this page is full. After page two is completed, post the entry to a new page before transferring any other journal entry to the Ledger. This process is explained in Chapter 28. The above example will guide you for this and similar entries.

After posting the entries to the Ledger and referencing the postings in the Journal, place "Jewels" in the Index at once. *Gioe* (jewels) will appear under the letters G or Z, depending on how it is pronounced. In Venice, it is customarily placed under Z (*Zioe*), while in Tuscany, under G. Therefore, you may place it under whichever you desire.

Chapter 16

How Entries Relating to Merchandise Should be Posted
to the Debit and Credit in the Ledger.

You will be able to transfer easily from the Inventory to the Journal four items of your personal goods; silver, linen, featherbeds, and clothing. These items of Inventory are not taken from the Memorandum, for the reasons stated in Chapter 6. The entries to be made in the Journal, the debit and credit posting in the Ledger, and the referencing of the accounts in the Index, I will leave to your ingenuity.

Only the seventh item of the Inventory, *mechini* ginger, will be entered in the Journal and in the Ledger. This should be sufficient instruction to enable you to record all other items relating to your merchandise. Always keep in mind numbers, weights, measurements, and values, in accordance with the different ways that it is customary to do business in Rialto, and different geographical locations. It is not possible to give you full examples of all such transactions, but from the few which are given here, you will be able to handle any special cases. If you were to require me to give you an example of the way in which business is transacted in Trani, Lecce, Bari, Betonto, in Marca and in our Tuscany, including the names of merchandise, weights, measurements, brands, etc., this volume would be too large. On the contrary, I intend to conclude it with brevity.

In order to enter the ginger in the Journal, say as follows:

Debit *Mechini* Ginger in bulk or packages (you may say it as you like), credit ditto (by which is understood Capital, because it has already been mentioned in the entry immediately preceding, in which you entered the second item, pertaining to Jewels). I possess on this day so many packages weighing so many pounds. They have a current value per hundred, or by the pound, of so many *ducats*, the total of which amounts to so many *ducats*. Value:
L. . . , S. . . , G. . . , P. . . .

After entering it in the Journal in this manner, cancel it in the Memorandum or Inventory as was done for the other items. For this entry and all others in the Journal, always place two entries in the Ledger, the first as debit and the second as a credit. In posting the debit entry from the Journal to the Ledger, proceed in this way: First, always place the year at the top of the page if it is not already there, but not the day. It is not customary to put down the day at the beginning of pages of the Ledger, because on the same page there may appear several debit and credit entries which belong to the same year but refer to different days and months. Even if on the same page there were only one cash or some other kind of entry, the day appearing at the top of the page would be of no use. This is because it is necessary to write down the various transactions that take place by their different days and months. It is for this reason that businessmen never put down the day at the top of the pages in Ledgers, since they do not see the least justification for it.

Debit the Ledger as follows:

> Debit *Mechini* Ginger in bulk, or so many packages, on November 8th, credit Capital for so many packages weighing so many pounds, in my store or at my house, which according to current prices I value at so many *ducats* per hundred, the total of which amounts to so many *ducats*, page 2.
>
> L. . . , S. . . , G. . . , P. . . .

Then cancel this entry on the debit side of the Journal. Then make the credit posting to Capital.

> On the same day, credit Capital, debit *Mechini* Ginger, in bulk or packages, page 3.
>
> L. . . , S. . . , G. . . , P. . . .

After it has been so entered, you shall cancel the entry on the credit side of the Journal and write down in the left margin of the Journal the numbers of the respective pages of the Ledger, one above the other. Place the three above and the two below, because the debit entry is posted on page 3, and the credit entry on page 2 of the Ledger. You will immediately enter it in the Index under its respective letter, which may be G or some other letter for the reason given in the preceding chapter.

Chapter 17

The Keeping of Accounts With Public Offices,
and the Municipal Loan Bank in Venice,
Which Is Governed by Districts.

I will not give you additional rules regarding other items such as leather goods for coverings, tanned, raw, or fine. Enter them one by one in the Journal and Ledger, carefully writing down and cancelling everything in proper order without forgetting anything. The businessman must understand things better than the butcher.

If you carry on business with the Venetian Municipal Loan Bank, or other banks as in Florence or the *Monte delle Dote* in Genoa, or other offices or bureaus, you should always keep your accounts very carefully. Have good written evidence of debits and credits in the handwriting of the clerks. Carefully remember this advice for reasons which I will explain to you later in the chapter on documents and letters.

These offices often change their clerks. Since each likes to keep the books in his own way, he always blames the previous clerks for not keeping the books in good order. They are always trying to persuade you that their way is better than all the others. For this reason, they sometimes mix up the accounts of these offices in such a way that they do not correspond with anything. It will be a woeful experience if you have anything to do with these people. Therefore, deal as carefully with them as you would with those at home, and have a chief watch your employees at the store. Though they all may show ignorance, perhaps they carry out their work in good order.

You will be able to keep accounts in this way with the Gabellari and Datiari (revenue officers) regarding such things as you buy and sell, plant and grow, etc. It is customary in Venice for people to keep large accounts through the Offices of Exchange: Some at 1%, some at 2%, and some at 4%.

Mention the particular broker's book through which the business transaction was made, and also the special mark which he has in his book: The book (called *Chiamans* in Venice) is that in which a record is kept of any business transactions at the Office. Each broker has a book, or a place in some book, in the Office in which he keeps a record of all the business transactions which he has had with citizens or foreigners. If the broker should not carry out his work properly, he would be penalized and dismissed.

The High Signoria of Venice punishes them and their clerks who do harm. I remember many who in past years were severely punished. It is right to have an officer whose sole duty is to oversee all these offices and determine whether the books are well or poorly kept.

Chapter 18

How to Keep Your Accounts With the Office of Exchange
in Venice. How to Make Entries Relating Thereto
in the Memorandum, Journal, and Ledger.
Information About Loans.

When you want to do business with the offices, debit the Municipal
Loan Bank so much per cent on all kinds of Capital deposited with them,
noting the pertinent district. Do similarly for the amount of your daily
sales for there are many transactions made for you and for others. Carefully note to whom the goods are sold and their places of business, as
do those people who know and who are familiar with the customs of
the Rialto. When you withdraw funds, always credit the bank, day by
day and district by district.

In doing business with the Office of Exchange, keep the account in
the following manner: When you buy any merchandise through their
brokers, credit the Office 2%, 3%, or 4% of the whole amount, and
debit it to the particular merchandise obtained. It is necessary that the
buyer always retain the proper percentage from the seller, in cash or
otherwise, as the Office does not concern itself with anything except
the amount to which it is entitled. The brokers make a report of the
transaction (how, for what, and with whom it was made) in order to
have clear evidence in case any question should arise.

A common proverb says: "One who does nothing makes no mistakes; one who makes no mistakes does not learn."

If the parties wish to settle any question, they would examine the
record of the transaction made by the broker. To this record, according
to public decree, full faith is given as to a public document made by a
notary. The Office of the Consuls very often issues its judgments according to it.

Therefore, when you buy anything, you must always know the

brokerage due the Exchange. Withhold one-half of this from what is due to the seller (the seller's share). For example, if the particular merchandise that you buy is subject to a 4% payment to the Office (as per public decree of the Republic), retain 2% of what you have to pay the seller. Having deducted that amount, he will receive the balance due him. You then owe the Office for the entire brokerage due them, debiting the amount to the goods you have purchased, and crediting the Office in your Ledger.[8] The Office, as I have said, is not concerned with the seller, but with the purchaser.

The buyer has the right to withdraw merchandise from official warehouses in proportion to the brokerage paid to the Exchange. Whether it is desired to withdraw goods daily or in another fashion, the amount to be taken must be verified by the books kept at the counters.

So as to know how much merchandise they can take out, businessmen must keep a careful account with the Office. They are not permitted to withdraw more than the proportionate percentage of the brokerage paid (unless they have paid extra brokerage to the Office).

I will give you an example of these purchases and how transactions with the Office must appear in the Journal and in the Ledger.

First, express yourself in the Memorandum as follows:

> I (or we), on the day above mentioned, have purchased from Mr. Giovanni Antonio, of Messina, so many loaves and boxes of Palermo sugar weighing (without boxes, wrappings, ropes, and straw) so much, at so many *ducats* per hundred, amounting in total to so many *ducats*. I deduct Mr. Giovanni Antonio's share of the brokerage due the Exchange at the rate of so much per cent, so many *ducats, grossi, picioli*. Mr. Giovanni de Gaiardi was the broker. Net value totals so many *ducats, grossi, picioli*, paid in cash.

The same transaction would be entered in the Journal in the following manner:

> Debit Palermo Sugar, credit Cash. The cash was paid to Mr. Giovanni Antonio of Messina, for so many boxes and so many loaves

---

[8] For example, assume goods cost 100 *lire*. The goods would be debited with 98 *lire* (net of the seller's share of the brokerage), and the seller credited with 98 *lire*. The second entry would debit the goods with 4 *lire*, and credit the Office with 4 *lire* (the seller's and buyer's share of the brokerage).

60

weighing (without boxes, wrappers, ropes, and straw) so much, at so many *ducats* per hundred, amounting in total to so many *ducats*. I deduct Mr. Antonio's share of the brokerage due the Exchange at the rate of so much per cent, so many *ducats*, etc., leaving the net amount of so many *ducats*. The broker was Mr. Giovanni de Gaiardi. *Value:*

$$L. . . , S. . . , G. . . , P. . . .$$

In the Ledger make the entries as follows:

Debit Palermo Sugar on a certain day, credit Cash. Paid cash to Mr. Giovanni Antonio, of Messina, for so many boxes and loaves, weighing net, so much, at so many *ducats* per hundred, which amounts to so many *ducats*, page 1.

$$L. . . , S. . . , G. . . , P. . . .$$

Credit Cash with a like amount in the opposite manner. Always credit the Exchange with twice the amount which you retain from the price paid to the seller: The commission due by him together with your equal share.

After recording this, make another entry immediately, crediting the Office with the total commission and debiting the merchandise. This is a sufficient example for purchase by cash. Now consider a transaction made partly by cash and partly on time.

First, in the Memorandum, say as follows:

By cash and on time, on a certain day, I have purchased from Mr. Giovanni Antonio, of Messina, so many loaves of Palermo Sugar, at a net weight of so much, at so many *ducats* per hundred, amounting in total to so many *ducats*. I deduct his share of the brokerage due to the Exchange at so much per cent, so many *ducats*. As part payment, I have paid so many *ducats*, and for the rest I shall have time to pay until the end of August next. The broker was Mr. Giovanni Gaiardi. Value totals so many *ducats*, *grossi*, *picioli*.

You need not have a written copy containing the terms of the transaction, because the broker's record at the Office is sufficient. However, as a precaution, some people require it.

The entries shall appear in the Journal as follows:

First, credit Giovanni Antonio for the total amount, and then debit

61

him for the amount which he has already received. Second, record the entry describing the original transaction.

Debit Palermo Sugar, on November 8th, credit Mr. Giovanni Antonio, of Messina, for so many loaves, weighing net so much, at so many *ducats* per hundred, making a total of so many *ducats*. I deduct his share of the brokerage due the Exchange at so much per cent, so many *ducats*, leaving the net balance of so many *ducats*, of which I now pay so much, and the balance due at the end of next August. The broker was Mr. Giovanni Gaiardi. *Value:*
L. . . , S. . . , G. . . , P. . . .

Immediately after, credit the Office of Exchange for the commission due it.

Debit Palermo Sugar, credit Office of Exchange, for the amount above mentioned, so many *ducats* at the rate of so much per cent for my share, and so much per cent for Mr. Giovanni Antonio's share, amounting in total to so many *ducats, grossi, picioli. Value:*
L. . . , S. . . , G. . . , P. . . .

For the cash payment, debit him and credit Cash in the Journal as follows:

Debit Giovanni Antonio, of Messina, credit Cash. Paid cash to him as part payment for Palermo Sugar, and so on according to the terms of the transaction, so many *ducats*, as it appears on his receipt written in his own handwriting. *Value:*
L. . . , S. . . , G. . . , P. . . .

The debit of the purchase transaction shall appear in the Ledger as follows:

Debit Palermo Sugar on November 8, credit Giovanni Antonio, of Messina, for so many boxes and loaves, weighing so much net, at so many *ducats* per hundred, amounting to so many *ducats*, net of brokerage, due the Exchange, page 4.
L. . . , S. . . , G. . . , P. . . .

The same item shall be credited in the Ledger as follows:

Credit Mr. Giovanni Antonio, of Messina, on November 8th, debit Palermo Sugar for so many loaves, weighing so much net, at so many *ducats* per hundred, amounting to so many *ducats*, net of brokerage due to the Exchange, of which I must now pay so many *ducats*, and the balance at the end of next August. The broker was Mr. Giovanni de Gaiardi, page 4.

L. . . , S. . . , G. . . , P. . . .

For the cash payment, post the debit to the Ledger as follows:

Debit Mr. Giovanni Antonio, of Messina, on November 8th, credit Cash. Paid cash to him as part payment on sugar which I received from him according to our agreement as is shown by his own handwriting in his book, page 1.

L. . . , S. . . , G. . . , P. . . .

The brokerage account of the Exchange shall appear in the Ledger as follows:

Credit Office of Exchange, November 8th, debit Palermo Sugar. Sugar was purchased from Mr. Giovanni Antonio, of Messina, at so much per hundred, amounting to so many *ducats*. The broker was Mr. Giovanni de Gaiardi, page, etc.

L. . . , S. . . , G. . . , P. . . .

Chapter 19

How to Make the Entries in Your Principal Books for the
Payments Which Have to be Made by Draft
or Through the Bank.

The foregoing should be sufficient to guide you for purchases, whether payment is made:

1. Wholly in cash,
2. Wholly through the bank,
3. Wholly by draft,
4. Wholly by goods,
5. Wholly on time,
6. Partly cash and partly through the bank,
7. Partly in cash and partly by draft,[9]
8. Partly cash and partly goods,
9. Partly in cash and partly on time,
10. Partly through the bank and partly by draft,
11. Partly goods and partly through the bank,
12. Partly through the bank and partly on time,
13. Partly goods and partly by draft,
14. Through any other combination of the bank, cash, draft, and goods.

It is customary to make purchases in all these ways. Enter them first in the Memorandum, then in the Journal, and finally in the Ledger.

When you make a payment partly through the bank and partly by draft, deliver first the draft and then settle through the bank. This is much safer. Many observe this precaution even when payment is to

[9] This alternative was not contained in the listing in Chapter 9 of the nine customary ways to make purchases. Paciolo also omits from this listing items 7 and 8 in Chapter 9 (partly goods and partly on time, and partly by draft and partly on time).

be made partly by cash, instead of first settling the balance through the bank. If you make payments partly through the bank, partly goods, partly by draft, and partly cash, debit the seller with the total of these and credit the individual items, each in its own place. If you should purchase by any other method, handle the transactions in a similar way.

Now that you understand the procedure for purchasing, you will also understand what to do when selling to others. In this latter case, debit the different buyers, and credit your merchandise. Debit Cash if you get money or Drafts if you get drafts in payment, and credit Drafts when they are paid by the bank. That is how to handle those transactions in an orderly manner. Referring again to the discussion on purchases, credit the purchaser with all which he gives you in payment.

This will be sufficient instruction on this subject.

Chapter 20

The Well Known and Peculiar Entries in Business for
Trading and Partnership and How They Should be Entered
in the Business Books. Simple Tradings and Dates,
Then Complex Tradings, Examples of Each in the
Memorandum, Journal, and Ledger.

Certain peculiar and well known entries will now be illustrated. In business it is desirable to arrange some of these separately from the others, so that their respective profits and losses can be readily seen. These entries cover tradings, partnerships, journeys made on your behalf, your own private journeys, commissions received from others, drafts or bills of exchange, and store accounts. In what follows, I will tell you clearly about these accounts, and how to enter them in your books in an orderly way, so that you make no mistake in your affairs.

First, I shall show you how to enter a trade.

Trades are usually of three kinds, simple, complex, and on time. Therefore, no matter how you record a trade in your books, describe it first in detail in the Memorandum, how it was carried out and whether it was made through a broker.

After it has been described in this way, place a money value on the particular goods in accordance with the current value of the things you have given. Use whatever kind of money you desire in the Memorandum. It does not matter which you choose, because the bookkeeper later transfers the entry to the Journal and Ledger and reduces the amount to the standard money which you have adopted.

If you do not enter the value of the things you have traded, you cannot, without great difficulty, learn from the books and accounts what your profit or loss is.

You may desire to keep specific account of the goods received in trade, for this will enable you to know how much profit or loss was made on each separate lot. This would help you know which were the best transactions.

You also may keep all similar goods under one account. For example, if you already have some ginger, and you received some more through a trade, make the entries in the Journal as follows:

Debit *Bellidi* Ginger in bulk or package, credit Sugar, of a certain kind, so many packages, weighing so much. Ginger was received in exchange for sugar in this manner: I valued the sugar at 24 *ducats* per hundred, provided that I would receive one-third payment in cash. I valued the ginger at so many *ducats* per hundred for which I should give so many loaves of sugar, weighing so much, worth 20 *ducats* per hundred if paid for in cash. For the said ginger, Mr. Trader received so many loaves of sugar. *Value:*
L. . . , S. . . , G. . . , P. . . .

If you do not always know the exact number of loaves of sugar which you have given for the ginger, do not be concerned. In the following entry you may correct that which is short. Since you know exactly the weight and the money value of sugar, the number of loaves can be corrected in the Cash entry. It is not always possible to keep account of all small details.

With regard to whatever cash you received, debit Cash and credit Sugar in the following manner:

Debit Cash, credit Sugar. I received cash in trade from Mr. Trader, for a certain number of loaves of sugar, weighing so much. *Value:*
L. . . , S. . . , G. . . , P. . . .

If you do not want to keep separate accounts, similar items should immediately be recorded in the Journal under the Merchandise Account. However, if you want to keep a separate account in the Journal, make the entry this way:

Debit *Bellidi* Ginger received in trade from Mr. Trader, credit Sugar, etc. (state here everything, continuing as before).

In the Ledger, then, there would be separate accounts. This should suffice for other trades, which you will be able to handle without further explanation.

Chapter 21

The Well Known Account Called Partnership.

Another well known account deals with partnership or joint ventures. A joint relationship may exist for any reason with other people in any trade, such as cloth, silks, spices, cotton, dyes, and exchanges. These partnership capital accounts must be entered separate from your own in each of the three books.

In the Memorandum, after writing the date at the top, state in a simple way all the details of the partnership. Such a statement should include the terms and conditions of the partnership, referring to documents or other instruments that might have been made between the partners. It should set forth:

1. How long the partnership is intended to exist.
2. Its objectives.
3. The employees or apprentices to be employed.
4. The partners' shares.
5. How much each invests in the business (and whether in goods or cash).
6. The debits and credits assumed by the partnership.

You should, one by one, credit each of the partners for the amount which he contributes to the business, debiting Cash with the same amount if you keep the account among your own. But if you keep this Cash account separate from your own, you will be able to carry on partnership business more clearly. This is particularly true if you are the head of the business, in which case you should have a separate set of books.

It would facilitate things for you if you could keep accounts in the same books, opening new accounts separate from all the others. I will show how you must enter them concisely in your Memorandum, and then in your own Journal and Ledger. If you keep separate books, I will not give you further instruction, because what I have said before is sufficient to guide you in all your business. Make the following entry in the Memorandum:

On this day I entered into a partnership contract with Mr. *A* Partner and Mr. *B* Partner for dealing in wool. The terms and conditions of the partnership appear in writing in such-and-such instrument and are binding for so many years. Mr. *A* Partner contributed so much cash; Mr. *B* Partner contributed so many bales of French wool, weighing net so much, and valued at so many *ducats* per bushel. Mr. *A* Partner also contributed so many debtors, namely, Mr. *A* Receivable for so many *ducats*, and Mr. *B* Receivable for so many. I contributed so many *ducats* as my share, making a total of so many *ducats*.

In the Journal enter each item in its proper place, identifying your Partnership's Cash and your Partnership's Capital. For every entry that you may make, identify the accounts of the partnership so that you can distinguish them from your own private entries. First, make the Cash entry, and then follow systematically with the other entries:

Debit Partnership Cash, credit Mr. *A* Partner's Capital account. (If he had other accounts with you they will not get confused as long as you identify). Mr. *A* Partner contributed this day so much cash as his share, according to our agreement as appears in the written documents. *Value:*

$$L. . . , S. . . , G. . . , P. . . .$$

In this manner, mention the other things which they have contributed:

Debit Partnership French Wool, credit Mr. *B* Partner's Capital account for so many bales, weighing net in total, at so many *ducats* per bushel, according to the terms of the contract or document we have entered into. In total they are worth so many *ducats*. *Value:*

$$L. . . , S. . . , G. . . , P. . . .$$

Proceeding with the other items, you shall enter the assigned debtors as follows:

Debit Mr. *A* Receivable and Mr. *B* Receivable—Partnership account, credit Mr. *A* Partner's Capital account. According to our agreement, Mr. *A* Partner contributed so many debtors, amounting in total to so many *ducats. Value:*

$$L. \ldots, S. \ldots, G. \ldots, P. \ldots$$

Now that you have been introduced to these new entries, I will not extend myself any further, as in the beginning of this treatise I pointed out that everything could not be treated. Nor will I say anything about the way in which these entries should be made in the Ledger, because it is easy to know which items should be entered as debits, and which as credits. Enter them in the same manner as described in Chapter 15; cancel them in the Journal as indicated in Chapter 12; place in the margin just opposite them the debit and credit page numbers of the Ledger; as they are entered in the Ledger, enter them also in the Index.

Chapter 22

The Entries for Each Kind of Expense; for Example,
Ordinary and Extraordinary Household Expenses,
Business Expenses, and Wages of Clerks and Apprentices.

In addition to the accounts spoken of so far, you shall also have these in your books: Business expenses, ordinary and extraordinary household expenses, and petty cash. You shall also have an account for profit and loss, or as you may say, increase and decrease, profit and damage, or gain and loss. These accounts are necessary to every business so that the businessman will always know what his capital is, and at the end of the period, how it is progressing. I will illustrate clearly how these entries should be made.

The account Business Expense is kept because every small item cannot be recorded in the merchandise account. This is true because you will sometimes have further expenses in paying porters, weighers, packers, shippers, drivers, and others, paying to one a *soldo*, to another two *soldi*, etc. If you kept separate accounts it would be too lengthy and not worth the expense. As the proverb says: "Officials do not bother with details."

You may also use those same people (drivers, porters, shippers, and packers) for different kinds of things. While employing them for loading or unloading different kinds of merchandise at a seaport, they will be paid for all these services at one time, and you could not readily charge the different kinds of merchandise separately. You therefore open this account called Business Expense, which always carries a debit balance, as do all other expenses. Salaries of shop clerks and apprentices can also be entered in this account, although some keep a separate account so that they know how much they pay for salaries annually. This account should never have a credit balance. Should such be the case, there would be a mistake in the books. Therefore, say as follows in the Memorandum:

On this day we paid to drivers, shippers, packers, weighers, etc., who loaded and unloaded certain goods, so many *ducats*.

Then in the Journal it will be necessary to say as follows:

Debit Business Expense, credit Cash. Cash was paid for shipping, carriage, weighing, and packing, for certain goods, so many *ducats* in total. *Value:*
L. . . , S. . . , G. . . , P. . . .

In the Ledger you shall state as follows:

Debit Business Expense, credit Cash on this day, etc., page, etc.
L. . . , S. . . , G. . . , P. . . .

The account for ordinary household expenses is absolutely necessary. It will include such expenses as grains, wines, wood, oil, salt, meat, boots, hats, expenses for tailoring, woolen clothes, drinks, tips, barbers, bakers, water-carriers, kitchen utensils, vases, glasses, and all the buckets, baths, tubs, and casks. Many people keep separate accounts for these things, so that they can see at a glance how each one stands. You may not only keep accounts for these things, but with any other accounts that you desire. However, I will show you what the businessman cannot do without.

You shall keep the Household Expense account in the same way that I have told you to keep the Business Expense account, making each entry day by day as large expenses such as grains, wool, and wines occur. Again, many people open separate accounts for these different things, enabling them to find out easily at the end of the year (or from time to time) how much has been paid out for a certain thing.

For such small expenses as meat, fish, and expenses of the barbers, set aside one or two *ducats* in a little bag, and make small payments out of this amount. It would not be possible to keep account of all these small things. In the Journal say as follows:

Debit Household Expenses, credit Cash. Cash was set aside in a small bag for small expenses, so many *ducats*. *Value:*
L. . . , S. . . , G. . . , P. . . .

You may include in the household expenses all extraordinary expenses which do not occur in the ordinary course of business. That which you spend in playing various kinds of games, or for things or money which you might lose, or that might be stolen, or lost at sea or through fires; all of these are classified as extraordinary expenses. You may keep separate accounts for them in order to know clearly at the end of the year how much you have spent as extraordinary expenses. Such an account should also include gifts and presents that you might give to anyone for any reason. I will speak of these expenses no longer, because I am sure that you will be able to handle them better than you would have before.

Putting this subject aside, I will speak of how to enter your store accounts in the Ledger and in the other books, for if you want to keep them yourself, it is a very nice thing for you to know. You must pay close attention.

Chapter 23

The Order and Manner in Which the Accounts of a Store
Should be Kept. How the Entries Should be Made
Separately in the Authentic Books of the Owner
and Those in the Store.

If you have a store apart from your house which receives its daily supplies from your house, keep your accounts in this way: For the daily goods which you supply the store, debit the store in your books, and credit the merchandise which you supplied, item by item. Imagine that the store is a person who owes you the amount you supply it or spend for it for any purpose. On the contrary, credit it with everything you take out of it or receive from it, as if it were a debtor paying you little by little. Therefore, you may see whether the store is operating at a profit or a loss, and know what to do and how to manage it.

Some store owners debit the manager of the store in their books. However, this should not be done without his consent, because you should never enter any person's name in your books as a debtor without his knowledge. Nor may a creditor, under any condition, be entered without his consent. If you should do these things, you would be wrong and your books would be considered false.

As to the fixtures which you might put in the store, which are necessary for running it according to its peculiar requirements, debit them to the store, or to the person who manages it. In the case of a drugstore, you would have to furnish it with such things as vases, boiling pots, and copper utensils with which to do the work. The manager of the store should take an inventory of the fixtures in his own handwriting, or have someone appointed by him to do it. In this way, everything shall be clear. This is sufficient information for accounting for a store whose management you have placed in the care of someone else, or to one of your employees.

However, if you wish to manage the store yourself, account for it in the following manner and all will be well. Suppose that you do all of your business through the store and do not have to manage any other business. If this were the case you would keep the books as I have said before, whether buying or selling. Credit those who supply you with goods on time or credit Cash if you buy for cash, and debit the store accounts for the purchase. If you sell at retail and the sales do not amount to more than four or six *ducats*, keep these monies in a small box. After eight or ten days take out such proceeds and debit the total amount to Cash, and credit the pertinent store accounts with the total. The entry will credit the various merchandise sold (for which you shall have kept an account. I shall not talk at length about this because I have given you sufficient explanation previously).

Now you will be able to understand how to do your accounting, for accounts are nothing else than the expression in writing of the proper order of your affairs: You will know all about your business and whether or not it is going well. As the proverb says: "He who does business without knowing all about it, sees his money go like flies." According to the state of your business, you will be able to remedy that which is required. This is sufficient on this subject.

Chapter 24

Posting the Entries With the Bank in the Journal and Ledger. Bills of Exchange—Whether You Deal With a Bank or as Banker With Other Persons. Receipts for Drafts—What Is Understood by Them, and Why They Are Made Out In Duplicate.

When you do business with banks such as those found in Venice, Bruges, Antwerp, Barcelona, and certain other well-known business centers, you must diligently keep your accounts with them. It is common practice to deposit your money with the bank for greater security, or leave it as a deposit in order to make your daily payments therefrom to Peter, John, and Martin. A bank draft is like a public notarial instrument, because it is under the control of the Dominion.

If you put money in the bank, debit the bank or the owners or partners of the bank and credit Cash, making the entries in the Journal as follows:

> Debit Bank of Lipamani, credit Cash for cash deposited with the Lipamani Bank by me, or by others for my account, on this day, in gold or other money which amounts in total to so many *ducats.*
> *Value:*
> $$L. . . , S. . . , G. . . , P. . . .$$

For greater security, have the banker give you an acknowledgement in writing. If you make other deposits on the same day, get another receipt. In this way, things will always be kept clear.

Sometimes this kind of receipt is not given, because the books of the bank are always public and authentic. Yet, it is better to require a receipt for security, because things are never too clear for the businessman.

It makes no difference whether you keep your account with the bank in the name of the owners or the partners. Nor does it matter if you open the account under the name of the bank (as in the manner shown above) for it is the same as if you opened it under the names of the owners or partners. If you keep it under the name of the owners, you will say as follows:

> Debit Mr. Girolimo Lipamani, banker, and associates (if there is more than one), credit Cash, etc. (and complete the entry).

Always make note in your books of all agreements, terms, and conditions that might arise, including written instruments and the places where you keep them (whether file box, pouch, trunk, etc.), so that they may be easily found. These documents should be kept diligently as the permanent record of the transaction because of the dangers which may arise.

Since you may have several different business relations with the bankers (for yourself or for others), always keep separate accounts with them so as not to mix one thing with another. This would cause great confusion. In your entries say: "On account of a certain thing, or on account of Mr. Martino, or on account of merchandise, or on account of money deposited in your own name or in the name of others," which entries I know you will be able to handle. Proceed in the same way if others should remit money to you for some account. Debit Cash (the bank) for that amount, stating whether it was in part payment or in full, and credit the person that gave you the money for that amount. In this way, all will be correct.

When you withdraw money from the bank to pay somebody else or to make remittances to others in other countries, do just the opposite of what has up to now been said. If you withdraw money, debit your Cash and credit the bank or its owners for the amount withdrawn. If you order payment through the bank to somebody else, debit this party and credit the bank or its owners for that amount, stating the reasons for such payment. For the former case, say in your Journal as follows:

> Debit Cash, credit Bank (or Mr. Girolino Lipamani) for cash which on this day or some other day I withdrew for my needs in total so many *ducats. Value:*
>
> $$L. . ., S. . ., G. . ., P. . . .$$

If you should order payment in favor of Mr. Martino, for instance, say:

Debit Martino of a certain place, credit Bank for so many *ducats* for which I ordered payment on this day, in part or in full or for a loan. *Value:*

$$L. . . , S. . . , G. . . , P. . . .$$

Always transfer these entries from the Journal to the Ledger, enter them in the Index, and cancel them in the Memorandum and Journal.

The same method should be used when remittances or withdrawals are made elsewhere, such as London, Bruges, Rome and Lyons. Mention in the cover letter the terms and conditions, and whether these drafts are at sight or at a certain date, or payable at the pleasure of the payee. Also mention whether it is a first, second, or third draft. This should be done so that no misunderstanding can arise between you and your correspondent. Mention what kind of monies you draw or remit, their value, the commission, expenses, and the costs and interest that might occur following a protest, so that the terms of the transaction will be recorded. Proceed in this way when dealing with a bank.

On the contrary, suppose that you are the banker, carrying on in the opposite way. When you pay, debit the particular person to whom payment is made and credit your Cash. If your creditor (without withdrawing money) should order payment to somebody else, say in the Journal: "Debit that particular creditor, credit the person to whom the money was assigned, etc." In this manner, make the transfer from one creditor to another, while still remaining debtor. By so doing, you act as a go-between (as witness and agent of the parties). For your ink, paper, rent, trouble, and time you get a just commission, which is always lawful. This is true even though there is no risk of loss in travel through a draft, since you do not assume the degree of risk associated with transferring money to third parties, as in exchange transactions.

If you are a banker and you close an account with your creditors, always ask that they return all the papers, documents, notices, or other writings in your own hand-writing that they might have. Whenever you prepare any such documents, always mention it in your books. Consequently, when the time comes you will remember to ask for their

78

return and destroy them, so that nobody else should afterwards appear with them and claim money again on the same documents.

Always require proper receipts. You might, for instance, come from Geneva to Venice with a draft on Messrs. Giovanni Frescobaldi and Co. of Florence, which might be for payment at sight or on a certain date, or at your pleasure, for 100 *ducats* (for as many *ducats* as you have paid the drawer of the draft). Then, when the said Messrs. Giovanni and Co. honor the draft and pay you the said sum, they will require you to give two receipts written in your own handwriting. (If any parties to such a transaction do not know how to write, a third party or notary would make them out). They will not be satisfied with one receipt because they must send one to the banker at Geneva, who wrote them to pay the 100 *ducats* to you for his account in order to show that they have honored his request. For this reason, they will send a receipt written in your own handwriting. They will keep the other receipt on file for their own use, so that when they settle accounts with the other banker he could not deny the transaction. If you should return to Geneva you would not be able to complain about him or Messrs. Giovanni and Co., for if you should, he would show you the receipt written in your own handwriting and you would be embarrassed. All these precautions should be taken because of the bad faith of the present times.

Out of this transaction two entries should be posted to the Ledger: One entry to the account of Mr. Giovanni, debiting the drawer of the draft, and the other entry in the account of your correspondent in Geneva, crediting Mr. Giovanni with the 100 *ducats*. The receipt which you gave them for their payment on the draft is the basis for these entries.

This is the method which all the bankers of the world use so that their transactions may appear clear. Therefore, in spite of the trouble on your part, post everything in its place with great care.

Chapter 25

The Income and Expense Account, Which Is Usually Kept in the Ledger.

Some people keep an account called Income and Expense in their books in which they enter extraordinary items or any other things they deem proper. Others keep an account for extraordinary expenses to enter any gifts that they may give or receive. This account has both debits and credits, including what they give, receive, and keep. At the end of the period, when all pertinent accounts are closed, they transfer the balance of the account to Profit and Loss. The balance of the latter is then transferred to Capital, as will be illustrated in Chapter 32.

Actually, the Household Expenses account is sufficient for all this unless someone would like to keep a separate account of every minute thing to satisfy his own curiosity (even to a bootlace tip). However, this would serve no useful purpose, as things should be summarized when possible.

In some areas, it is customary to keep the Income and Expense account in a separate book which is balanced when the authenticated books are balanced. This custom should not be criticized, but it requires more work.

Chapter 26

How Entries Relating to Trips Should be Made in the
Business Books. Why, of Necessity, There Are
Two Ledgers for This.

Trips are usually made in two ways, either by yourself personally or by someone else acting in your behalf. Therefore, this gives rise to several ways of keeping the accounts for trips. Duplicate books should always be kept, whether you are making trips personally or someone is traveling in your behalf. One Ledger is kept at home and the other taken on the trip. If you go on a trip yourself, you must make an Inventory of the items that you take with you. You must also prepare a small Journal and small Ledger and take them with you, following the above-mentioned methods.

If you sell, buy, or exchange goods, debit and credit the appropriate person, goods, cash, traveling capital, traveling profit and loss, etc. This is the clearest way, no matter what other people may say.

You might keep an account for the firm furnishing you the goods that you take with you on a particular journey. In this case credit the firm and debit the different goods one by one in the small Ledger, thus opening your merchandise accounts and your Capital account, in as orderly a manner as you would in your main books.

On your safe return, send back to the firm money or the goods taken in exchange for those that they had given you. You would then close your accounts with them, entering the respective profit or loss in the correct place in your big Ledger. In this way your business will be clear.

However, if the trip is made by someone else in your behalf, debit this party with all the goods entrusted to him, saying, "Debit trip entrusted to Mr. Salesman, etc." Keep an account with him for all goods and monies as though he were one of your customers. He will make up a small Ledger in which he credits you for everything. When he returns, he will settle his accounts with you, and if your traveler were wrong, (you have a basis for correcting his accounts).[10]

[10] Paciolo did not complete this sentence; we added the phrase within the parenthesis.

Chapter 27

The Well Known Account Called Profit and Loss, or Profit and Deficit. How This Account Should be Kept in the Ledger, and the Reason Why It Is Not Placed in the Journal as the Other Accounts.

After all transactions have been recorded, one additional account should be opened, which is named in various localities, the Profit and Loss, Profit and Damage, or Increase and Decrease account, into which all other accounts in the Ledger must be closed. Entries to this account should not be made in the Journal, but only in the Ledger. They differ from other entries in that they originate from debit and credit balances in the accounts and not from exchange transactions.

Make entries in the account as follows: "Debit Profit and Loss, and credit Profit and Loss." For example, if you had sustained a loss in a particular line of goods as evidenced by the Ledger account having a debit balance, add enough to the credit so as to make the debit and credit equal. Then make the following notation in the merchandise Ledger account: "I debit Profit and Loss that which I credit here in order to balance the loss sustained, etc." Record the page of the Profit and Loss account to which you transfer the entry. Then debit the Profit and Loss account saying as follows: "Debit Profit and Loss, on a certain day, for so much loss sustained by a particular line of goods, which has been credited to that merchandise account, in order to balance it, page so-and-so."

If the account of this particular line of goods would show a profit instead of a loss, as witnessed by a credit balance, proceed in the opposite way.

Make profit and loss entries in this manner for all goods or other accounts, whether they show good or bad results. In this way, your Ledger will always show the accounts in balance, as much debited as credited. This is how the Ledger will be found if it is correct. You will also be able to see at a glance whether you are gaining or losing, and how much.

The Profit and Loss account will then be closed and transferred into the Capital account, which is always the last in all Ledgers. It is consequently the receptacle of all other accounts.

Chapter 28

How Ledger Accounts Should be Carried Forward When They Are Full. The Place to Which the Remainder Should be Transferred, in Order to Avoid Fraud in the Ledger.

When an account has been filled and you cannot enter any more debit or credit items, you must immediately carry this account forward to a place behind all the others. Leave no space in the Ledger between this transferred account and the last of the other accounts. To do otherwise would indicate fraud in the book.

Proceed in a manner similar to that given when closing accounts to Profit and Loss. In making the transfers between accounts, post the debit or credit balances in the Ledger only, because transfers should not appear in the Journal. It would be permissible to enter transfers in the Journal, but it is not necessary. It would amount to trouble without benefit. All you have to do is to increase the side of the account which has the smaller balance, that is, if the account has a debit balance, add the difference to its credit. Here is an example to give you a clear idea.

Suppose that Martino has carried a long account with you of several transactions, so that his account must be transferred from page 30 of your Ledger. Suppose further that the last account of your Ledger is at the top of page 60, and that on the same page there is room enough to transfer the Martino account. Suppose that his account shows a debit total of *L.* 80, *S.* 15, *G.* 15, *P.* 24, and a credit sum of *L.* 72, *S.* 9, *G.* 3, *P.* 17, (showing what he has given you). The debit total exceeds the credit total by *L.* 8, *S.* 6, *G.* 12, *P.* 7, which sum you should bring forward to the debit side of the new account, adding the same amount in the credit column of the old account to make it balance, saying as follows:

> On a certain day, credit Martino. I carry forward a debit balance of *L.* 8, *S.* 6, *G.* 12, *P.* 7, as remainder, and enter the same amount here to close the account, page 60.
>
> *L* 8, *S* 6, *G* 12, *P* 7

Then cancel the old account on both the debit and credit sides with a diagonal line. After that, go to page 60 and enter the debit balance, always writing at the top of the page the year if it has not already been done. You shall enter there the following:

> Debit Martino on a certain day, credit Martino for the debit balance taken from the page of his old account therein entered in the credit to close. Page 30.
>
> $$L\ 8,\ S\ 6,\ G\ 12,\ P\ 7$$

Transfer all accounts in the same manner, placing them in such a way that no spaces are left whatsoever in between. Accounts should always be opened in the original order of place, day and date in which they arise, so that nobody can slander you.

Chapter 29

How to Change the Year in the Ledger Between Entries
When the Books Are Not Closed Every Year.

You might have occasion to change the year in your Ledger accounts before you balance the books. In this case, write the year in the margin just above the first entry of the new year. All the entries which follow will be understood as having taken place during that year.

However, it is always a good idea to close your books each year, especially if you are in partnership. As the proverb says: "Frequent accounting makes for lasting friendship."

Chapter 30

How to Abstract an Account for a Debtor or an Employer
if You Are the Manager or Agent for the
Administration of His Property.

In addition to other documents already mentioned, it is necessary to know how to make an abstract (or statement) of account for your debtor, in case he should request it. This request cannot reasonably be refused, especially if he has had an account with you for a long time. Begin at the time of the first transaction, or in the event that you have had previous settlements, at any other point in time where your debtor may desire. You should do this willingly.

Record all the entries into one account on a sheet of paper large enough to contain them. If they cannot all be entered on one side, carry the balance forward to the other side of the sheet. Continue until you have recorded all of the entries, then reduce them to the debit or credit balance that the account should show. These statements of account must be made out diligently.

The foregoing is the method you would use in reconciling your accounts with that of your clients. However, if you were to act as an agent for others under powers or orders, you would make out a statement in a similar manner for your employer. This would be done in the same order as it appears in the Ledger, crediting yourself from time to time with your commissions according to your agreements. Then at the end, make yourself his debtor for the balance, or his creditor if you had advanced any money or goods of your own. Your employer will then compare your statement with his own books, and if he finds it correct will like and trust you more. For this reason, keep an orderly account in your own handwriting of everything which he has given or sent to you.

On the other hand, if you are an employer, you might have your agents, clerks, etc., make out these statements for your clients. Before these statements are delivered, however, they should be carefully compared with each entry in the Ledger, Journal, and Memorandum, and with any other documents referred to therein, so that no mistake can arise between the parties.

Chapter 31

How to Correct One or More Entries in a Place
Different From That in Which They Should Have Been.
This Usually Happens Through Absentmindedness.

The good bookkeeper should know how to correct, or deviate as it is
called in Florence, an entry which he may have posted by mistake in
the wrong place. For example, if he had entered it as a debit when it
should have been a credit, this would be on the wrong side; or made
an entry in the account of Giovanni, when it should have been entered
in the account of Martino, this would be in the wrong place.

At times you cannot be so diligent as to avoid mistakes. As the proverb says: "He who does nothing, makes no mistakes. But he who makes
no mistakes, does not learn."

Correct erroneous entries in the following manner. For example, if
the entry had been debited when it should have been credited, make
another entry opposite this one in the credit for the same amount saying as follows:

> On a certain day, the amount which has been debited opposite
> here, should have been credited on this page.
> $$L. . . , S. . . , G. . . , P. . . .$$

The above entry will be for the amount which was posted by mistake in the debit column. Make a cross or other mark in front of these
two entries, so that when you make a statement of account you will
leave these entries out. After posting the correcting entry in the credit
column, it is just as if you had not written in the debit column. Then
make the entry in the credit column where it should have been, and
everything will be as it should.

Chapter 32

How the Ledger Should be Balanced and How the Accounts of the Old Ledger Should be Transferred to the New Ledger: the Manner of Verifying It With Its Journal, Memorandum, and Other Documents.

Having noted well the foregoing, attention can now be given to carrying forward the accounts from one Ledger to another when you want to have a new Ledger. This happens when the old Ledger is filled up or because of the beginning of a new year. In the best known places, such as Milan, the big merchants customarily close their Ledger every year.

Carrying forward the accounts to a new Ledger, together with those operations which shall follow, is called "balancing the Ledger." If you want to do it well and in an orderly way, it will require diligence. Do it in the following manner: First, try to get a helper for it is difficult to do alone. Give the Journal to him for greater precaution, while keeping the Ledger for yourself. Then, beginning with the first entry in the Journal, tell him to call out the numbers of the Ledger pages where the entry should have been posted, first the debit, then the credit. Always find the page in the Ledger that he calls and check to see that the entry (the kind, for what, whom, and the amount) he calls is the same. If it is the same, say so. Finding that it is the same in the Ledger as in the Journal, mark it off by checking or dotting it or placing any proper mark over the *lire* mark, or elsewhere, so that it can readily be seen. Ask your helper to make this mark (the one you use depends largely on the custom of your locality) in the Journal at the same entry. Take care that neither of you marks an entry without the other doing so, as great errors might then arise. Once an entry is marked it is assumed to be correct.

The above procedure is also done in making out statements of account for your debtors. Before you deliver them, they must be compared with the Ledger, Journal, and any other place in which the entries or details of the transaction may have been recorded.

Having proceeded in this manner through all the accounts in the Ledger and Journal, and having found that the debit and credit entries correspond, it will mean that the entries are properly placed and correct.

Take care that your helper shall mark each entry in the Journal with two checks, dots, or other marks, while in the Ledger, you will make only one for each entry. This is because for every entry in the Journal there are two made in the Ledger.

In checking the balance in the Journal, it is well to place the two checks or dots over the *lire* (one beneath the other). This will indicate that both the debit and credit entries in the Ledger are correct. Some people put a mark before *Per* for the debit, and after *lire* for the credit. Either way is satisfactory. One single mark in the Journal (only the debit mark) might do if you also mark the credit on the page of the Ledger where that entry is. This procedure can be used because the credit page is mentioned in the corresponding debit posting in the Ledger, which will direct you at once to the appropriate pages. It would then not be necessary for your helper to call to you this credit page, since when comparing only the debit side with the Journal, you can check the credit side in the Ledger yourself. But it would be more convenient if you proceeded with your helper in the manner earlier detailed.

After finishing the checking of the Journal you find some account or entry which has not been checked off in the debit or credit in the Ledger, a mistake in the Ledger has been made. A superfluous debit or credit entry has been posted, and you should correct this error at once by posting a similar amount on the opposite side. If the superfluous entry was on the debit side, you would make a similar entry on the credit side and vice versa, thus making everything correct.

Should your helper find some entry in the Journal which is not found in the Ledger, an error in the Ledger has occurred. A correction should again be made, but in a different way. Immediately debit and credit the unposted entry to the Ledger, explaining the difference in the dates, for the entry would be made at a date much later than it should have been. A good bookkeeper should always mention these differences and why they arise, so that the books are above suspicion. When this is done, the good notary in his instruments will be unable to criticize what might have been added or omitted. The good bookkeeper should act in this way, so that the firm's reputation will be maintained.

If the said entry should have been posted only in the debit or only in the credit, it would be sufficient to place it immediately on the particular side where it was missing, explaining that it was left out by mistake. In this manner, all your accounts will have been adjusted; if they agree, you will know that your Ledger is correct and well kept.

Sometimes entries are found in the Ledger which have not been checked to related entries in the Journal, because they cannot be found in the Journal. These represent the balances posted to the debit or to the credit to close accounts carried forward. The correlative entries in the Ledger relating to these balances will be found on the page numbers indicated in these accounts. Finding the related entries in their proper places, you may conclude that your Ledger is in proper order.

That which has been said so far about comparing the Ledger with the Journal should also be observed in comparing the Memorandum with the Journal. This should be done day by day if you use the Memorandum in the manner illustrated at the beginning of this treatise. If you have other books, do the same. However, the last book to be compared is the Ledger, and the next-to-last, the Journal.

Chapter 33

How to Record the Transactions That Might Occur
While Balancing the Books. Why No Entry Should be
Changed or Made During That Time in the Old Books.

After you have ascertained that the entries in all the books are correct, see that no new entry is made in the old books of original entry, the Memorandum and the Journal, or postings to the Ledger. This is because the closing is assumed to be accomplished on the same day. Should some transactions occur while the books are being balanced and closed, enter them in the new books of original entry. However, do not post them to the Ledger until the balances from the old Ledger have been carried forward.

If a new set of books is not yet available, record these transactions, their respective dates, and their explanations on a separate sheet until the new books are ready. When they are ready, enter the items in these books which bear a new mark (if the books just closed were marked with a Cross, mark the new ones with the letter *A*).

Chapter 34

The Way to Close All the Accounts of the Old Ledger.
The Preparation of the Trial Balance, Which Totals All
of the Debits and Credits.

Having verified the accuracy of the books, close the Ledger accounts
in this way: Commence with the Cash account, then Accounts Receivable (debtors), then Merchandise, etc. Transfer the balances from these
accounts to the new Ledger. Do not, as was stated above, enter the balances in the Journal.

Summarize all the accounts with debit and credit balances, always
adding to the lesser side the amount to be carried forward, just as if
the balances were being carried forward to a different page in the same
Ledger. In this case, balances are carried forward from one Ledger to
another. The page reference placed in the old Ledger refers to the page
on which the balance appears in the new Ledger, so that in the transfer from one book to another, the accounts are entered only once in
each Ledger. This is unique to the last entry in the accounts of the
Ledger.

Make the transfer as follows: Suppose that Mr. Martino's account
has a debit balance in your Ledger ✠ at page 60 of *L* 12, *S* 15, *G* 10,
P 26, and it is to be transferred to page 8 of Ledger *A*. Credit his account
in Ledger ✠ at the end of all other entries as follows:

> Credit Martino, on a certain day, debit himself posted in Ledger
> *A* for the balance which is added here to close his account, page 8.
> *Value:*
> $$L \ 12, \ S \ 15, \ G \ 10, \ P \ 26$$

Then cancel the account in both the debit and the credit with a diagonal line, as you were taught in the bringing forward of accounts. Then

place totals at the foot of both the debit and credit columns, so that the account will appear equal at a glance.

In debiting Ledger A, after first putting down the year at the top of the page, and placing the day in the body of the posting (for the reason stated in Chapter 15), say:

> Debit Martino of a certain place, on a certain day, credit himself for the balance transferred from Ledger ✠ and posted to the credit thereof to close, page 60. *Value:*
>
> L 12, S 15, G 10, P 26

Proceed in this manner closing all the accounts of Ledger ✠ which you intend to transfer to Ledger A: Cash, Capital, Merchandise, Personal and Real Property, Accounts Receivable (debtors), Accounts Payable (creditors), and accounts with offices, brokerage houses and public weighers (with whom long accounts are sometimes carried). Those private expense accounts which you may not care to transfer to Ledger A, and which do not have to be given account of to someone else, should be closed in the same Ledger (Ledger ✠) to Profit and Loss, or Increase and Decrease, or Profit and Damage (as it is sometimes called). Accounts such as Mercantile Expenses, Household Expenses, and all Extraordinary Expenses (rents, pensions, feudal tributes, etc.) would satisfy these criteria. Enter these in the debit column of Profit and Loss, for it would be rare indeed that expense accounts had credit balances; complete the closing by crediting the lesser side in the expense accounts. Debit the lesser side in income accounts, crediting Profit and Loss, by saying "Credit Profit and Loss in this Ledger on a certain page, etc." In this manner, all these different accounts will have been closed to Profit and Loss in Ledger ✠ . By summing the debit and credit entries to this account, the profit or loss will be known, for when the balance is derived in this account, the balance in all the accounts will be known. The items which had to be deducted were deducted, and the items which had to be added were added. If this account should show a debit balance, that amount will have been lost in your business since you began or previously closed your books. If it carried a credit balance, that amount has been gained during the period.

After seeing what your profit or loss is by the balance in this account, close and transfer this balance into the Capital account in which, at the outset of your business, was recorded your Inventory in its entirety. The Profit and Loss account shall be closed in this way: If the loss exceeds the profit (May God protect each of us who is really a good Christian from such a state of affairs), then credit the account in the usual manner: "Credit Profit and Loss on a certain day, debit Capital for loss sustained in this account, on a certain page. Value, etc." Then cancel the account, debit and credit, with a diagonal line as previously stated, also placing debit and credit totals at the bottom of each column, which totals should be equal. Then debit the Capital account:

> Debit Capital on a certain day, credit Profit and Loss for the loss credited to Profit and Loss account in order to close on page so-and-so. *Value:*
> $$L. . . , S. . . , G. . . , P. . . .$$

If, instead, there should be a profit (when Profit and Loss has a credit balance), debit it for an amount sufficient to close it. Indicate the page of the Capital account to which the balance in Profit and Loss is to be transferred. Credit the same amount to Capital on the same side in which all other personal and real possessions have been entered. From the Capital account, therefore, which is always the last account in the Ledger, you may learn the entire value of your property. The value of your business appears in the Capital account as the net of all debits and credits transferred to Ledger *A* as well as the other accounts closed into Profit and Loss and then into Capital.

Then the Capital account in Ledger ✠, along with the other open accounts, should be closed and carried forward to Ledger *A*, either in total or entry by entry. Although it can be done either way, it is customary to transfer the total amount so that the entire value of your business appears to you at a glance.

Do not forget to number the pages of Ledger *A* before entering the different accounts in the Index in their proper places. In this way accounts may easily be found when needed. Everything in the old Ledger, with its Journal and Memorandum, will be closed.

So that everything regarding the closing will be clear, summarize all the debit totals that appear in Ledger ✠ at the left of a sheet of paper, and all the credit totals at the right. Then sum all of the debit items (which is called the grand total), and likewise total all of the credit items

97

(which is also called the grand total). The first is the grand total of the debits, and the second the grand total of the credits. Now if the two grand totals are equal, you may conclude that the Ledger was well kept and closed, in line with the reasons stated in Chapter 14. However, if one grand total exceeds the other, it would indicate an error in the Ledger. This error must be searched out diligently with the intellectual ability God has given you, and with the help of what you have learned. As was said in the beginning, it is very necessary for the good business-man to do his part of the work. If you cannot be a good accountant in your business, you will grope your way forward like a blind man and may meet great losses. Therefore, with deep study and care, make all efforts to be a good accountant. I have shown you how to become one easily, having duly provided all the necessary rules in their proper places. Everything may be found by means of the table of contents placed at the beginning of this work.

In Chapter 12, I promised to give you a summary of the most essential things in the present treatise. This will cover those things discussed up to this part and will no doubt be very useful.

Remember to pray to God for me that I may proceed by always doing well to His praise and glory.

Chapter 35

*How and in What Order Manuscripts, Confidential Letters,
Policies, Processes, Judgments, and Other Important
Instruments Should be Kept. The Registry
of Important Letters.*

The manner and order for keeping documents, such as manuscripts of payments made, receipts for drafts or merchandise given, and confidential letters follows. These things are of great importance to businessmen of high esteem, and there is considerable risk of losing them.

First, with regard to confidential letters received from customers, keep them in a small desk until the end of the month. At the end of the month, tie them in a bundle and put them away, writing on the outside of each letter the date of its receipt and the date of your reply to it. Do this every month. At the end of the year, tie up all of the bundles into a large one, writing the year on it, and put it away. Whenever a letter of that particular year is required, go to this bundle.

Keep pouches in your desk in which to place letters given to you by your friends to be sent away with your own. If a letter is to be sent to Rome, put it in the Rome pouch, and if to Florence, in the Florence pouch, etc. Then, when sending the messenger, put these letters with your own and send them to your correspondent in that certain place. To be of service is always a good thing.

It is also customary to give a gratuity to the messenger in order to be served well. The messenger wears a belt with several pockets for carrying letters. This belt has as many pockets as there are places in which you do your business, such as Rome, Florence, Naples, Milan, Genoa, Lyons, London, and Bruges. On each pocket write its correct destination: Write Rome on one, Florence on another, etc. Put the letters which have been given to you by your friends to send to those places in their respective pockets.

When answering a letter or sending letters for others, note on the outside of the letter which was answered by whom the reply was sent, for whom it is intended, on whose behalf it was sent, and the day of its departure.

Never forget to record the date in all your transactions, whether they are large or small. Be especially careful to record it in letters, in which should always be placed the year, the day, the place, and your name. It is customary for businessmen to place their names at the end of the letter in the right hand corner, with the year, day, and locality at the top. But first, like a good Christian, remember to write down the glorious name of our Savior, the sweet name of Jesus (or in place of it, the sign of the Holy Cross), in whose name all business should be transacted as follows: "✠, 1494, on this 17th day of April, in Venice."

Then continue, "My dear . . ." Students and other people, such as monks and priests, who are not in business, usually place the day and year at the end of the letter. Confusion would surely arise if the day were not written, and people would make fun of you. This is because people say that the letter which does not bear the day was written during the night, and the letter which does not bear the place was written in the other world and not in this one. Besides the fun made of you, there would be confusion, which is worse.

After the letter has been sent, put the one which has prompted the reply in its proper place; what has been said of one letter applies to all others. Observe that when important letters are sent, they should first be recorded in a book maintained for this special purpose. In this book, copy verbatim the important letters such as letters of exchange, and letters relating to goods or money sent. If they are not of great importance, record only the pertinent information, saying: "On this day, we have written to Mr. Correspondent, and sent him certain things in accordance with his letter of a certain date, in which he requested or gave us a commission, etc., which letter we have placed in a certain pouch."

After sealing and addressing the letter, it is the custom of many to place their special mark on the outside. This is to show that it is the correspondence of a businessman, for whom there is great regard. As was said in the beginning of this treatise, businessmen are the ones who maintain the Republics.

To accomplish the same purpose, the Most Reverend Cardinals write their names on the outside of letters. In this way no one can claim that he did not know from whom the letter was sent. The correspondence of the Pope remains open so that its contents, such as bulls and privileges might be known. However, for certain things which are confidential, the "Fisherman's Seal" (Seal of St. Peter) is frequently used.

All of your letters should be bundled monthly and yearly, and filed in an orderly way in a safe cupboard or chest. File them in the order in which they are received during the day, so that they may be easily found if you need them. I need not speak further of this, for I know you understand it.

Keep manuscripts referring to accounts owed you by debtors in a more secret place, such as private chests or boxes. Similarly, keep receipts in a safe place for any emergency. However, when you pay others, have them write out a receipt in a receipt book, as I told you at the beginning so that a receipt could not be easily lost or mislaid.

The following must also be kept in safe and separate places: First, import policies (such as those of the well known brokers); second, notes of businessmen or weighmen; third, sealed documents for goods placed in or withdrawn from sea or land customhouses; fourth, judgments or decrees of consuls or other public officials; fifth, all kinds of notarial instruments written on parchment; and sixth, copies of instruments, papers, writings, etc., from attorneys or lawyers relating to lawsuits.

Note carefully in a separate book called the record book, those things which you might forget, and which would cause you loss. Do this daily. Every evening, just before retiring, glance through this book to see if everything that was to be done was, in fact, done. Cancel with a penline those things which have been done. Remind yourself also of those things which are entered as evidence of loans to your friends and neighbors for a day or two, such as shop vases, boilers, or other utensils.

These rules, together with the other useful ones previously given, should be followed. Expanding or contracting them according to the time and place is necessary for your purposes. It is impossible in business to give point by point rules about everything. As the proverb says, "More skills are required to make a good businessman than to make a good lawyer." Therefore, if you understand well all the things spoken of up to now, you will carry on your business affairs intelligently and well.

Chapter 36

The Summary of Rules and Ways of Keeping a Ledger.

1. All credits must be placed on the right-hand side of the Ledger, and all debits on the left-hand side.

2. All entries posted to the Ledger must consist of double entries, a debit and a credit.

3. Each debit and credit entry must contain three things: The date, the amount, and the reason for the entry.

4. The second or last name in the debit posting must be the first in the credit posting.

5. The credit posting shall be made on the same day as the debit posting.

6. A "Trial Balance" of the Ledger should be prepared by folding a sheet of paper lengthwise and recording the debit account balances on the left, and the credit account balances on the right. By summing, it is seen whether the debit balances equal the credit balances and whether the Ledger is in order.

7. The Trial Balance of the Ledger must be equal: The sum of the debits must be equal to the sum of the credits. Otherwise, there would be a mistake in the Ledger.

8. The Cash account should always have a debit balance or be equal. Otherwise, the account will be in error.

9. No one should appear as a debtor in your Ledger without his permission and consent. If he did, the account would be considered false. Similarly, terms or conditions cannot be added to the credit without the permission and consent of the creditor. If such were done, the account would be false.

10. The values in the Ledger must be recorded in one kind of money. It is permissible to name all sorts of money within the entry such as

ducats, denari, florins, gold *scudi,* or whatever, but in entering the amount in the money columns, use the same kind with which you began the Ledger.

11.   The debit or credit postings to the Cash account may be abbreviated, if you desire, by not giving the explanation for the entry. Say only, "Debit Mr. Seller of a certain place," or "Credit Mr. Buyer of a certain place." The explanation will be stated in the opposite related posting.

12.   If it is necessary to open a new account, use a new page without going back to previous pages, even if there were sufficient space. Never go back to write: Always go forward as the days go, which never return. If such were done, the Ledger would be false.

13.   If a posting were made to the Ledger by mistake (as sometimes happens through absentmindedness), and you wished to correct it, do as follows: Make a cross or other mark in the margin next to that particular posting, then make the posting on the opposite side in the same account. For example, assume that the wrong entry is a credit for L 50, S 10, D 6. Make the opposite entry saying, "Debit L 50, S 10, D 6, for the opposite entry marked with a cross which is hereby corrected. It should not have been posted at all." Then, mark the new posting with a cross.

14.   When an account is full such that no more entries can be made therein, and you want to carry forward that account balance, figure the balance in the account, whether debit or credit. Suppose that it is a credit balance of L 28, S 4, D 2. Then write on the opposite side, without mentioning any date, "Debit L 28, S 4, D 2, for the balance in this account posted in the credit at a certain page in this book." Mark next to this latter entry in the margin, R°, which means balance forward. It is not a true debit though it appears on the debit side. Rather, it is a credit balance transferred by way of a debit entry. Now keep turning pages until a new one is found, on which that account will be named and credited, without recording the day therein. Open the new account in the following manner: "Credit Mr. Seller of a certain place, L 28, S 4, D 2, with the balance of one of his accounts transferred from a certain page of this Ledger." Mark the entry in the margin, R°, (which signifies balance forward), and it is completed. Proceed in the same way if the

account shows a debit balance, what is entered on the credit side will be transferred to the debit side.[11]

15. When the Ledger is full or a new Ledger is to be opened, and you wish to transfer account balances into a new one, proceed as follows: First, see which sign appears on the cover of the old Ledger. If it is an *A*, the cover of the new book should be marked with a *B*, because all businessmen's books go into alphabetical order, one after another. Then take a trial balance of the old Ledger and see that it is equal and correct. Then copy into the new Ledger the debit and credit account balances in the order in which they appear in the trial balance. Make separate accounts for each debtor and creditor, leaving enough space to handle the volume of transactions that you anticipate. In each debit account balance to be entered in new Ledger *B*, say, "For so much debit balance on a certain page in the old Ledger marked *A*," and similarly for each credit account balance, "For so much credit balance on a certain page in the old Ledger marked *A*." This is the way to transfer the old Ledger account balances into the new one. In order to cancel the old Ledger, every open account shown on the trial balance must be closed. If an account in Ledger *A* has a credit balance (as the trial balance will indicate), it should be debited for the same amount, saying, "Debit for so much credit balance in this account which has been posted to the credit in new Ledger *B*, at a certain page." The old Ledger is closed in this way, and the new Ledger opened. Since I have shown you how to handle a credit balance, do the same for a debit balance, except in that case, credit the account which shows a debit balance and debit it in the new Ledger.

[11] This differs from Paciolo's instruction in Chapter 28. There he suggests that after the old account has been equalized, and the balance posted to the new, the old account should be cancelled "on both the debit and credit sides with a diagonal line."·This is his first mention of R° (*resto*-remainder).

Chapter 37

Items Which Should be Entered in the Ledger.

For all the cash which you find properly belongs to you, debit Cash and credit your Capital. Include amounts earned at different times in the past, bequeathed to you by deceased relatives, or given to you by some prince. All the jewels and merchandise which properly belong to you must be valued in cash, and kept separate one from the other. Make as many accounts in the Ledger as there are items, debiting each one saying: "Debit a certain thing, credit your Capital for so many of a certain thing which I have on this day, valued at so many *denari*, etc., credit posted at a certain page." Then credit your Capital account with the amount of these entries. Note that these entries should not be of less than 10 *ducats* each, for small things of little value are not entered in the Ledger. All the real property that you own such as houses, lands, and stores, shall be entered in the Ledger. Debit such properties separately with a cash value placed on them at your discretion, and credit your Capital account. As I told you in the rules, every entry requires these things: The date, the cash amount, and the reason for the entry.

If merchandise or any other thing is purchased for cash, debit the item purchased, and credit Cash. If you should say, "I bought that merchandise for cash, but a bank (or friend) will furnish the cash," debit the merchandise as stated above. However, instead of crediting Cash, you should credit that bank (or friend) who furnished the cash.

If merchandise or any other thing is purchased on time, debit the item purchased and credit the person from whom you made the time payment purchase.

If merchandise or any other thing is purchased partly for cash and partly on time, debit the merchandise and credit the person from whom you bought it. List the agreed-upon conditions. Suppose that you gave him one-third in cash and promised the rest in six months. If this is the case make the foregoing entry first, then debit the person from whom you made the purchase for the amount of cash given him (one-third), and credit the person or the bank which might have paid the cash for you.

All sales of merchandise or any other thing shall be dealt with as above, except that such transactions should be entered in the opposite way. Where I told you to debit Merchandise when purchasing it, you would credit Merchandise when selling it. Debit Cash, if it is sold for cash, or debit the bank that might have guaranteed the payment. If the sale were made on time, debit the person to whom you sold the merchandise. If the sale were made partly for cash and partly on time, enter it as I have shown you in the preceding two paragraphs which dealt with purchases on time.

If merchandise is sold by exchange, for example, you say, "I have sold 1,000 pounds of English wool in exchange for 2,000 pounds of pepper." I ask you, how should this entry be made in the Ledger? Do as follows: Estimate the cash value of the pepper, at your discretion. Suppose you place it at 12 *ducats* per hundred, or 240 *ducats* for the 2,000 pounds. Credit the English wool for 240 *ducats*, the amount for which you have sold it. This is the procedure to be followed in all exchange entries. Since 2,000 pounds of pepper valued at 240 *ducats* have been received, debit Pepper on this day, on a certain page, etc.

If loans of cash are made by you to some friend, debit your friend and credit Cash. If some friend loans you cash, debit Cash and credit your friend.

If you have received 8, 10, or 20 *ducats* to insure a ship, galley, or some other thing, debit Cash and credit 'Ship Insurance,' explaining the what, when, where, and how of the transaction clearly and fully, and at how much per cent.

If merchandise is consigned to you for sale or exchange on commission, and you pay transportation, duty, freight, storage, or other charges on the inventory, debit the account of the consignor and credit Cash.

Items Which Require Recording by Businessmen.

All household or shop chattels which you possess must be entered in proper order in the record book. Include separately all iron goods, leaving space to add other items, and sufficient space in the margin to indicate all those things which may be damaged, lost, given, or sold. However, it is not necessary to record chattels of little or no value in this book.

Record separately all brass and tin goods and such items made of wood, copper, silver, and gold, always leaving some blank pages on which to place additional items. In the case anything is missing, leave margins to give notice of this fact.

Record very clearly all of the particulars of the securities, obligations, or promises made to another, as well as goods or other things left in your custody (or for your use or loaned to you) by some friend. Do this also for all the things you have loaned to your friends.

All conditional dealings, both buying and selling, must be recorded. An example of this would be a contract specifying that if you send me by the next galleys returning from England, so many pounds of mixed wool, on condition that it is good and acceptable, I will give you so much per hundred weight, or send you so many pounds of cotton.

All the houses, lands, shops, or jewels rented out at so many *ducats* or *lire* per year, shall also be recorded. When the rent is received, that cash must be entered appropriately in the Ledger. If jewels, gold, or silver table services were loaned to some friend for 8 or 15 days, the particulars must not be entered in the Ledger, but in the record book. This is because they will be returned in a few days. In the same way, if things of a similar kind were loaned to you, they should not be entered in the Ledger, but noted in the record book.

An Illustration of Ledger Postings.

How Debit Entries Should be Posted	How Credit Entries Should be Posted
MCCCCLXXXXIII	*MCCCCLXXXXIII*
Debit Cash in Simone's name, (who is the son of Alessio Bombini) on November 14, 1493. Credit Francesco, (who is the son of Antonio Cavalcanti). Francesco made payments to us, the agent, for the account of Simone. The credit is posted on page 2.	Credit Francesco (the son of Antonio Cavalcanti) on Nov. 14, 1493. Debit Cash in Simone's name (who is Alessio Bombini's son). The debit and explanation is found on page 1.
Value: *L 62, S 13, D 2*	*Value:* *L 62, S 13, D 2*
Debit Ludovico, (son of Pietro Forestani) on Nov. 14, 1493. Credit Simone's Cash account for cash we loaned for him to Ludovico. Credit posted on page 1.	Credit Simone's Cash account on Nov. 14, 1493. Debit Ludovico (son of Pietro Forestani). Debit and explanation posted on page 3.
Value: *L 44, S 1, D 8*	*Value:* *L 44, S 1, D 8*
Debit ditto, on Nov. 18, 1493. Credit Martino (son of Forabaschi) for the amount which we, the agent, promised to Martino on behalf of Ludovico. Credit posted on page 4.	Credit Martino (son of Pietro Forabashi) on Nov. 18, 1493. Debit Ludovico (son of Pietro Forestani). Debit and explanation posted on page 3.
Value: *L 18, S 11, D 6*	*Value:* *L 18, S 11, D 6*

MCCCCLXXXXIII

Debit Martino (son of Pietro Forabaschi) on Nov. 22, 1493. Credit Simone's Cash account for the amount we paid to Martino on behalf of Ludovico. Credit is posted to Cash on page 1.
Value: *L* 18, *S* 11, *D* 6

MCCCCLXXXXIII

Credit Simone's Cash account on Nov. 22, 1493. Debit Martino (son of Pietro Forabaschi). Debit and explanation on page 4.
Value: *L* 18, *S* 11, *D* 6

Debit Francesco (son of Antonio Cavalcanti) on Nov. 22, 1493. Credit Ludovico (son of Pietro Forestani) for part payment of the amount which we, as agent, promised to Ludovico on behalf of Francesco. Credit posted on page 3.
Value: *L* 20, *S* 4, *D* 2

Credit Ludovico on Nov. 22, 1493. Debit Francesco. Debit and explanation posted on page 2.
Value: *L* 20, *S* 4, *D* 2

SECTION III

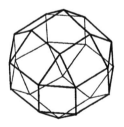

The Original Treatise
Reproduced

Comments on the Reproduction

Paciolo's bookkeeping treatise is reproduced in this section. It consists of 28 pages of text plus a title page. The title page is from the second edition of the SUMMA; the 1494 SUMMAS were not published with a title page. As can be seen by the page numbers at the top right hand side of Paciolo's treatise, it was customary to number only every other page.

Both SUMMAS were published using loose metal type. Although printing from carved blocks of wood had been done for centuries, loose metal type had been in use for only about thirty years when the 1494 edition was published. Gutenburg, the famous German printer, perfected this technique in the 1460's. By the late 1400's, many printers had fled or moved to Italy, where Venice and Florence flourished as printing centers.

Paciolo's SUMMA, especially the second edition, is considered to be one of the most beautiful examples of the printers' art of that era. Therefore, in addition to being collected by scholars of mathematics and accounting, the SUMMA is sought after by bibliophiles interested in the history and development of printing. Ninety-nine copies of the 1494 SUMMA and thirty-six of the 1523 edition are known to exist.

The original SUMMA is approximately the same size as today's standard sheet of typing paper. Photographing it for reproduction, even with modern technology, is a difficult chore, for many pages have deteriorated and the 500 year old binding of the book does not permit it to be opened completely flat. Therefore, we must apologize for any pages or portions thereof which are not totally clear.

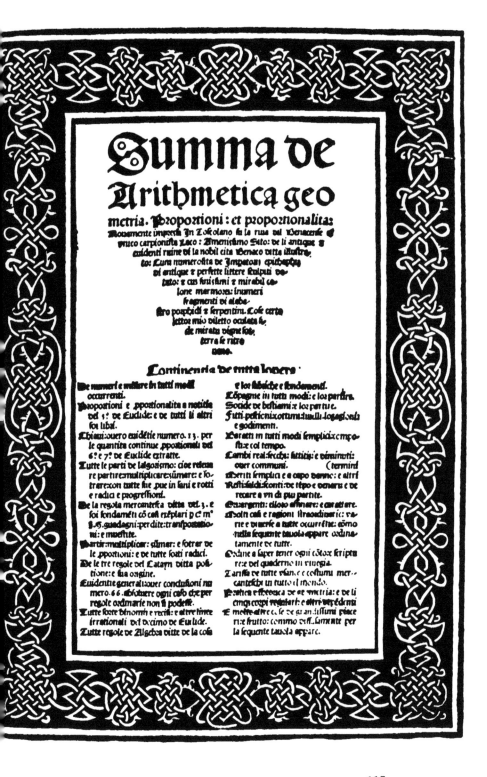

Summa de

Arithmetica geo

metria. Proportioni: et proportionalita:

Nouamente impressa In Toscolano fa la riua del Benacense
pruco carpionista Laco: Amenissimo Sito: de li antique e
euidenti ruine di la nobil cita Benaco tutta illustra:
to: Cum numerosita de Imperatori epithaphia
di antique e perfette littere sculpti: da
bato: e cun serissimi e mirabil co-
lone marmorea: inumeri
fragmenti di alaba-
stro porphidi e serpentini. Cose certa
lectore mio diletto oculata fi-
de mirata digne sob:
terra le nitre
nene.

Continentia de tutta lopera

De numeri e misure in tutti modi
occurrenti.

Proportioni e proportionalita a notitia
del 5º de Euclide: e de tutti li altri
soi libri.

Chiami ouero euidetie numero. 13. per
le quantita continue proportionali del
6º e 7º de Euclide extratte.

Tutte le parti de largorismo: cioe releua
re partire: multiplicare: sumare: e so-
trare con tutte sue pue in sani e rotti
e radici e progressioni.

De la regola mercantesca ditta del 3. e
soi fondameti cő cosa exemplari p c m°
$$-$ guadagni: per dite: transposatio-
ni: e modeste.

Partir: multiplicar: sumar: e sotrar in
le proportioni: e de tutte sorti radici.

De le tre regole del Cataym ditta posi-
tione: e sua origine.

Euidentie general: ouer conclusioni nu-
mero. 66. absoluere ogni caso che per
regole ordinarie non si podesse.

Tutte sorte binomii e recisi: e altre linee
irrationali del decimo de Euclide.

Tutte regole de Algebra ditte de la cosa

e lor sisiche e fondamenti.

Lopagnie in tutti modi: e lor partire.

Sotide de bestiami e lor parture.

Sutti pesti cni xortuma: tuutti: logagioni
e godimenti.

Baratti in tutti modi semplici e compo-
sta: col tempo.

Cambi real: secchi: fittitii: e diminuti:
ouer communi. (termini

Meriti semplici e a capo danno: e altri
Resti saldi: sконti de tepo e denari e de
recare a vn di piu partite.

Assignanti: di oro: affinare: e caratiare.

Assolti casi e ragioni straordinaric: va-
rie e diuerse a tutte occurrétie: como
nella sequente tauola appare ordina-
tamente de tutte.

Ordine a saper tener ogni cōtox scripta
ree del quaderno in riuegia.

Zarifia de tutte riane e costumi mer-
cantescbi in tutto il mondo.

Pratica e theorica de de metria: e de li
cinqi corpi regulari: e altri vsedimi

E molte altre cose de gra utilissimi piace
rie frutto: como sufficiente per
la sequente tauola appare.

Po mette pegno.10.contra.15.vnaltro mette.20.contra.27.dimandase chi che uantragio e quanto p c. Fa cosi prima uedi quanto meritaria.20.de scontro a rata.cbe.10.a.15.e dise.10.a.15.cbe bara.20.uirra bauer.30.donca uedi che non ba debito scontro babiando.27 oz uedi cbe li manca cbe li mãcbera da.27.a.30. cbe son.9.uedi cbe pte son de suo capital cbe e.·0.cbe son li.3̄₃.e tãto ebbe di dãno n l so ca pitale respecto a laltro.donca arguesci cbe laltro babia uãtagio li.3̄₅.del suo capitale cb uol dir.15.per.c°.cbe si troua ancbe a questo modo dicendo colui mettendo.10.tiraria.15.se me resse.100.cbe tirarauc.opera tiraria 150.qual salua.poi p laltro dirai se.20.uol.27.cbe uo ra.100.cbe uirra a uolere.135.cb uedi cbe manco cbe.150.del p°.si cbe ebbe suãtagio. El sape q̃to p c°.abbati.135.de.150.resta.15.e tãto ebbe dãno i tutto per bauer messo.100.cioe baue damno tal parte qual son.15.de.100.cbe son li.3̄₅.ut supza la'tro auanço p u cbe lui.15.in mite to cbe son li.3̄₅.pur de.100.suo capitale:sicbe auantagio.15.p.c°.fatta per cbe semp̃ tal par te quale pde luno qlla medesima preuene a nãçare laltro e cosi i baratti.

Tauola del Quaderno.

e quello che per lozo fe babia a denotare.   ca°.11
Del modo a faper ponere e dittare le ptite i lo gioznale del dare e de lauere cõ molti erem
pli:e de li doi altri termini nel quaderno ufitati luno detto caffa e laltro cauedale:e quello
che per effi fe babia intendere.   ca°.12
Del terço z vltimo libzo principale mercantefco detto el qderno commo debbe effer fatto e/
del fuo alfabeto cõmo fe debbia ozdinare vgniolo e dopio.   ca°.13
Del mõ a poztare le ptite del gioznale i qderno:e p che de vna i gioznale fe ne facia doi in q
derno:e del modo a depennare le partite in gioznale e de li doi numeri õ le carti del qua
derno che in le fue margine fi pone:e p che.   ca°.14
Del mõ a fape dittare le ptite de la caffa e cauedale nel quaderno i dare e bauere:e del mile/
fimo che di fopza nel pzincipio de la carta a lantico fi mette in effo:e de la fua mutatione:e
del cõpzir li fpacij de le carti fcõ le ptite piccole e grãdi fcõ el bifogno õ le facéde.ca.15
Cõmo fe debino dittare le partite de le mercantie che p inuentario o altro modo lomo fe ri
troua:nel quaderno in dare e in bauere.   ca°.16
Del modo a tener conto con li officij puplici:e per che:e de la camera delimpzeftitti in vene
tia che fe gouerna per via de fertieri.   ca°.17
Cõmo fe debia tener cõnto con lofficio de la meffetaria in uenetia e del dittare le fue par/
tire in memoziale:giornale:e qderno:e ancoza de limpzefti.   !ca°.18.
Del modo a fapere notare e dittare vna ptira õ robba cõpzata a cõtãti:i tutti.3.li libzi cioe me
moziale:gioznale:e quaderno:e cõme a pze cõtãti e pze tẽpo al medefimo Capitolo.
Cõnino fe debia ozdinare el pagamento che bauefle a fare per ditta e ba ndbo defcripta ne
li toi libzi pzincipali.   ca°.19
De le ptite famofe e pticulari nel maneggio traficãte cõmo fõno baratti cõpagnie zc.cõmo
le fe babbino afettare e ozdinare ne li libzi mercãtefchi:e pzima de li baratti femplici cõpo
fti e col tẽpo cõ apti e fẽpli de tutti i memoziale:giornale e qd erno.   ca°.20
De laltra partitta famofa ditta Compagnie:commo fe debino ozdinare:e dittare in tutti li
modi ocurrenti in ciafcunolibzo.   ca°.21.
De lozdine de le ptite de ciafcuna fpefa:cõmo de cafa ozdinarie:ftraordinarie:e di mercan
tia:falarij de garçoni e factori cõmo fabino a fcriuere:e dittare neli libzi.   ca°.22
De lozdine e mõ a fap tener vn cõto de botega in tua mano o adaltri recõmandata e cõmo
fe debino ne li libzi autentici del patrone e anche in quelli de botega feparatamente fcri/
uere e dittare.   ca°.23
Cõmo fe babino a fettare nel gioznale e qderno le ptite de li bachi de fcritta:eqli fe intredi/
no e doue ne fia:o de cãbi:tu cõ lozo ftando mercatante:e tu cõ altri quãdo foffe bachieri:
e doue fe quietãçe che p li cãbi fi fanno:e p che fe ne facia doi de medefimo tenoze.   ca°.24
De vnaltra partita che ale uolte fe coftuma nel qderno tenere detta entrata e ufcita e aleuolte
fenefa libzo particulare.e per che.   ca°.25
Cõmo fe babino afettare neli libzi le ptite de li uiaggi i fua mano:e qlle de li uiaggi recoma
dati:e cõmo de neceffita de tali nafcono doi quaderni.   ca°.26
De unaltra ptita famofa ditta pzo e danno o uero auançi e defauançi:commo la fabia a te
nere nel quaderno:e p che ella non fi metta nel gioznale cõmo le altre ptite.   ca°.27
Cõmo fe debino reportare in ançe le ptite nel quaderno:quando foffero piene:e i che luogo
fabbi a portare el refto:acio nõ fia pzefa malitia nel quaderno.   ca°.28
Del modo a faper mutare el milefimo nel quaderno fra le ptite che a la gioznata acafcano:
quando ogni anno non fi faldaffe li libzi.   ca°.29
Cõmo fe debia leuare vn conto al debitore che te domandaffe:e ancora al fuo patrone fi
ondo factoze e cõmeffo de tutta la aminiftratiõe de le robbe.   ca°.30
Del modo a ordine a faper retractare o uero iftoznare una o piu partite:che p error bauefle
pofte in altro luogo che doueffero andare cõmo aduene p 'memozagine.   ca°.31
Cõmo fe debia fare el bilancio del libzo e del modo a repoztare vn libro in laltro:cioe el q
derno vechio nel qderno nuouo e del modo a pontarlo con lo fuo giornale e memoziale e
altri fcontri dẽtro e difuoz del ditto quaderno.   ca°.32
Del modo e ordine a fcriuerele facende che occurreffero nel tempo che fi fa el bilancio:cioe
che fi faldano li libzi e commo neli li libri uedhi non fi debia fcriuere ne innouare cofa alcu
na in ditto tempo:e la cagione per che.   ca°.33

Commo fe debiano faldare tutte le partite del quaderno vecbio:e i cbi:e per cbe e de la fu
ma fumarum del dare e delauere ultimo fcontro del bilancio.						ca°.34
Del modo e ordie a faper tenere le fcripture menute cōmo fōno fcripti de mano lre familia
ri polixe:pceffi:fentērie e altri iftrumēti e del regiftro de le lettere iportāti.		ca°.35
Epilogo o uero fūmaria recolta de tutto el prefente tractato:acio con breue fubftātia fe ba
bia mandare a memozia le cofe dette.						ca°. 36

Diftinctio.nona.Tractatus.ti°.pticularis de cōputis z fcripturis.

De quelle cofe cbe fōno neceffarie al uero mercatante:e de lordine a fape bē tenere vn q̃/
derno cō fuo giornale i vinegia e ancbe p ognialtro luogo.		Capitolo primo.

Y reuerenti fubditi de.U.D.S.Magnanimo.D. acio a pieno
de tutto lordine mercantefco babino el bifogno:delibera i.Colt.
le cofe dinançe i q̃fta nra opa dicte) ancora particular tractato
grandemēte neceffario cōpillare.E in q̃fto folo lo iferto: p cbe
a ogniloro occurrēça el pfente libro li poffa fcruire.Si del mo /
do a conti e fcripture:cōmo de ragioni.E per effo intendo dar/
li norma fufficiente e baftante in tenere ordinatamente tutti lor
conti e libri.Pero cbe.(cōmo fi fa)tre cofe maxime fōno opor
tune:a cbi uole con debita diligētia mercantare.De le q̃li lapotif
fima e la pecunia numerata e ogni altra faculta fu' ftantiale.Ju
xta illud pl2y vnū aliquid neceffariozū è fubftantia.Sēça el cui
fuffragio mal fi po el manegio traficante exercitare. Auēga cbe
molti gia nudi cō bona fede cōmençando:de grā facēde babio fatto,E mediante lo credito
fedelmēte feruato i magne ricbeçe fieno peruenuti.Cbe afai p vtalia difcurrēdo nabiamo
cognofcdun. E piu gia nele grā republicbe non fi poteua dire:cbe la fede del bon mercatan
te.E a quella fi fermaua lor giuramento:dicēdo.A la fe de real mercatante. E cio nō deuef
fere admiratione:cōciofia cbe i la fede catolicamēte ognuno fi falui:e fença lei fia ipoffibile
piacere a dio.			La fecōda cofa cbe fi recerca al debito trafico:fie cbe fia buon ragionieri: e
pmpro cōputifta. E p quefto cōfequire.(difopra cōmo fe ueduto)dal príipio alafine: ba
uemo iducto regole e canoni a ciafcuna opatione requifiti.Jn modo cbe va fe:ogni diligē
te lectore.tutto potra iprendere.E cbi di quefta pte non foffe bene armato:la fequēte in ua
no li ferebbe.		La.3°.e vltima cofa oportuna fie:cbe cō bello ordie tutte fue facēde debita
mēte difponga:acio con breuita:poffa de ciafcūa hauer notitia:quanto alor debito e ancbe
credito:cbe circa altro non fatēde el trafico.E q̃fta pte fra laltre e alozo utiliffima:cbe i lor
facēde altramēte regerfe:feria ipoffibile:feça debito ordine de fcripture.E feça alcū repofo la
lor mēte fempre ftaria in gran trauagli.E po acio con laltre q̃fta poffino hauere.el pfente tra
ctato ordiai.Pel q̃le fe da el mō a tutte forti de fcripture:a ca°.p ca°.pcedēdo.E bē cbe nō
fi poffo cuff apōto tutto el bifogno fcriuere.Nō dimeno p q̃l cbe fe dira.El pegrino igeg̃a
q̃li caltro laplicara.	E feruaremo i effo el mō de vinegia:q̃le certamēte fra-g̃ialtri e molto
da cōmēdare.E mediante q̃llo i ogni altro fe porra guidare.E q̃fto dividerēmo b2.pti pn
cipali.Luna cbiamaremo iuētario.E laltra difpōne.E p².de luna:e poi de laltra fucceffiua
mēte fe dira fcdo lordie i la ppofta tauola contenuto.Per la q̃l facilmēte el lectore porra le
occur.rentie trouare fecondo el numero de fuoi capitoli e carti.

Dico lo debito ordie cbe fafpecta uol fap bē tenere vn q̃derno cō lo fuo giorna
le a q̃l cbe qui fe dira con diligētia ftia a tēto. E acio bē fintēda el .pceffo idurre
mo i cāpo vno cbe mo dinouo comēçi a traficare cōmo p ordie deba procedere
neltenere foi conti e fcripture:aciocbe fucitamēte ogni cofa poffi ritrouare pofta
al fuo luogo p cbe nō afertando le cofe debitamēte a li fuoi luogbi uerebbe i grandiffimi tra
uagli e cōfuffōi de tutte fue facēde.Jurta cōe dictū vbi nō è ordo ibi eft cōfufio.E pero a p
fecto docuēto dogni mercatante de tutto nfo .pceffo f aremo cōmo di fopra e ditto.2. pti
pncipali.Le q̃li apramēte q̃ fequēte cbiariremo:acio fructo falutifero fabia iprēdere. E pria
dimoftrando cb cofa fia iuētario e cōmo fabia fare e De la p² pte pncipale de q̃fto tractato
detta iuētario.E cbe cofa fia iuētario:e cōme fra mercanti fabia fare.	ca°.2	Lōuienfe
adonca p²imēte pfupponere e imaginare cbe ogni opante e moffo dalfine.E p poter q̃llo
debitamēte cōfeqre fa o gni fuo sforço nel fuo pceffo.vnde el fine de q̃lūcbe traficante e de
cōfequire licito e cōpetēte guadagno p fua fubftētatiōe.E pio fempre con lo nome de mefer
domenedio:debiano cōmençare lozo facende.E i nel p°. dogni lor fcripture:el fuo fancto

nome hauera mête zc.E po p².côuen che facia ſuo diligente iuêtario:i qſto modo.che ſem
pxe p².ſcriua in vn foglio o uero libzo va pxe.Lioche ſe ritroua hauer al môdo:de mobile:e
deſt abile.Lômençando ſemp va le coſe che ſôno in piu pgio e piu labili al perdere. Lômo
ſô li·ô.côtanti.Øioe. Argenti zc. per che le ſtabili Lômo ſôno.Laſi. Terreni.Lacune val-
le. pxſchiere e ſimili nô ſi poſſano ſmarire:cômo le coſe mobili.E ſucceſſiuamente poi de ma
no i mano.ſcriuaſe laltre. ponendo ſepxe p² el dizemileſimo:el luogo.el nome ſuo nel dicto
iuêtario.e tutto dicto iuêtario ſi deue tenere in vn medeſimo giozno:p che altramête varche
trauaglio nel mâegio futuro.E po a tuo exêplo:potre q vn pz n°.cômo ſe debia fare. per ſo
ql tu pte porrai i ogni luogo el ppoſito ſequire zc.vz.

Forma exêplare cô tutte ſue ſolennita in lo inuentario requiſite.   ca°.;

Al nome de dio.1493.a di.8.nouembxe in vinegia.

Queſto ſe quête ſi e lo iuêta. io de mi. Ø.va vine².de la côtrada de ſcô apoſtolo.
El qle ordenatamête io de mia mano ho ſcripto:o ro fatto ſcruere val tale zc.
De tutti li miei beni:Mobili e Stabili:Debiti:e Crediti che al môdo mi ritro
uo:fin qſto pſête giozno ſopra dito.p².pzita.   Jn p².mi trouo de côtâti fra ozo
e moneta:duc.tanti zc.Di qli tâti ſôno dozo venitiani.E tâti dozo ongari.E tâti.fio. larghi
fra papali:ſeneſi:e fiozêtini zc.Lauâço môete vargêto e raine de piu ſozti:cioe.Trôi. Ødar
celli.Larlini de rc.e de papa.E groſſi fiozêtini.Teſtoni milaneſi zc.z²   Jtê mi trouo i ço
ie ligate e deſligate. pezzi n°.tâti zc.De li qli tanti ſôno balaſſi i tauola ligati:i ozo ancili pe
ſano.ø.e caratti grani zc.luno o uero i ſûma.Qui poi dire a tuo mô zc. E tanti ſôno ſaſili
pur a tauola iſozmagli va dôna. peſano zc.E tâti ſôno rubi coculegni deſligadi peſano zc.
lialtri ſôno diamâti greçi a tauola:e pôridi zc. Ørrâdo le ſozti e peſi a tua uoglia.z² Jtê
mi trouo veſte de piu ſozte.tâte de la tale e tante de la tale zc.Ørrâdo ſuoi côditiôi. Lolo
ri:fodre e fogie zc.4². Jtê mi trouo argêti lauoran de.p. ſozti.Lômo tacçe bacili. Ræini.
Loſſleri. Pironi zc.E q narra tutto le ſozti a vna p vna zc.E peſa ciaſcuna lozza dapſe ſo
tilmête.E tiê côto de pezçi de peſi zc.de le legixe.E venetiana.Ø raguſea zc.E anche
ſtâpo.o uero ſegno che haueſſero farne mentiôe zc.5². Jtê mi trouo i ma ſſaria ô panni li
ni:cioe Lêçoli.Touagli.Lamiſe. Façi. li zc.Lapi n²tâti zc.leçuoli dc.3.zeli.Ødi.2.z.tele
padouane o altre zc.nuoui o vſati lôghi tanti bi. zc.E camiſe tante zc.touagle de re ie zc.fa
çuoli grandi n²tanti zc.E piccoli tanti zc.noui vſati zc.a tuo mô narra°le ſozti. 6². Jtez
mi trouo lecti ô piûa.n°.tanti zc.cô ſoi cauezali de piu² noua o ro vſata zc.federa noua zc.
qli perano i tutto.o ro vno p vno.8.tante zc.E eg°te del mio ſeg°.o dalt°.cômo ſi coſtu
ma zc. 7² Jtê mi trouo de mercantie i caſa ouer i magaçeni.zc.de piu ſozti.p².Lolli tan
ti de çêgari. michini peſano.8.ran°.zc.Segnati del tal ſeg°.zc.E coſi andarai narran°.a ſoz
ta p ſoz.ditte mercantie cô tutti côtraſegni ſia poſſibile.i cô q̂ta.piu chiareçça ſi poſſa.de pe
ſo n°.e miſura zc. 8² Jtê mi trouo colli tanti de çêgari bellidi zc.E cardi tâti de pip zc.
pip lôgo.o uer pip tôdo ſcôo che ſira zc. E fardi tanti di canelle zc.peſa°.zc.E colli tanti
garo².zc peſa°.zc.cô fuſti poluere e capelleti.o ro ſeça zc.E pezçi tâti.de vzçini zc.peſa°.zc.
e pezçi tanti ſan².roſſi o bianchi peſa°.zc.E coſi andarai mettêdo p ordie v°.ſotto laltro zc.
9² Jtê mi tr².pelami da fodre:cioe agnel°.bia²e albertôi puglieſi o marchiani zc.n°.tan
ti de la tal ſoz°.zc.e volpe mar°.n°tante côçe zc.e n°.tante crude zc.E camoçe côçe e tru
de zc.n°.tante zc. 10² Jtê mi trouo pelle ſi°.fo°.arme°.voſſi.vari.çebelini zc.n°.tanti de
la tal ſozte.E n°.tanti de la tale zc.Loſi deſtiguêdo a v².a v².diligêtemête con tutta verita:
acio el uero te habia a guidare zc. Auendo ſêp auertêça a le coſe che uâno a n°. E a qlle che
uâno a peſo.E a qlle cô vâno a miſura.po cô di qſte.3.ſoz².ſi coſtûa fare el trafico p tutto.
e alcune ſi mercatio a.Ø².Altre a.c°.altre a.8.altre a.ø.altre a n°.cioe a côto cômo pella
mi zc.altre a peçi.cômo çioie:e perle fine zc. Si che di tutte fa ben nota a coſa per coſa zc.
E queſte te baſtino a tua guida.Laltre per te poi ſequirai ſempre zc.   11². Jrem
mi trouo veſtabile pziam.vna caſa a tanti ſulari zc:a tante camere.Lozte. pozço. Ozto zc.
poſta in la contra de ſancto apeſtolo:ſora canale zc.apxeſſo el tale:e tale zc. Ønominando
li côfini:e referêdoti ali inſtriſe ui ſôno ârichi piu veri zc.E coſi ſe piu naueſe de le calci i di
uer ſi luoghi:nolarle a ſimili zc.12². Jtê mi trouo terreni lauoranui câpi.o uero ſtaioze. o
o uero panoza zc. Ønominâdoli ſcôo luſo del paeſe doue te troui.o uero doue ſôno ſituua
ti zc.n²tâti zc.Jnredêdo el câpo o uero ſtaioza de tauole tâte o câne o priche o beuolche zc.
poſti in la tal villa de padouana o altrode zc.Øpxeſſo li beni del tale zc.Lhiamâdo li cô
fini zc.E inſtrumêti.o uero pzita de cataſti.p li qli paghi[e fariôni i cômuno zc. Ønali lita
uora el tale zc.rêdano lâno de fitto cômûo:ſtara tâti e.ô.tâti zc.E coſi pte ua narâdo tu
tuoi poſſeſſiô zc. Øeſtiamiſoci°.13² Jtê mi tro°ba°ala came°.ô ipſli°. ouer alt°.môte iu²

Ducati tanti de caudale ñd fertier de canareggio 2c.O uero pte i vno fertieri e pte i vnal
tro.A arrando ancora i nome de chi fonno fcripti. E chiamando el libro de quello officio
El numero de le carti doue e la tua partita.El nome del fernuano che tien ditto libro:acio có
piu tua facilita ρ̃douai a fcotere li poffi trouar.Pero che in tali officij bifogna hauere mol
ti fcontri alcuolte per la gran multitudine che ci iteruiene 2c.E nota el milefimo che refpó
dano a tépo ρ tépo acio fappia quádo uengano li fo pro.e quáto per céto refpódino 2c. 14
Item in trouo debitori numero tanti 2c.luno e f tale del tale 2c.che me deue dare duca
ti tanti 2c.L altro e el tale del tale 2c. E cofi narrali a vno:a vno con boni contra fegni:e co
gnomi:e luoghi:e quanto te debano dare:e ρ che.E cofi fe ui fon fcripti de mã o iniftrumé-
ti de nodari fra noi fãne métione 2c.In fũma debo fcotere ducati tãti 2c.De boni ŏ.Se fi/
rà perfone da bene 2c.altramēti dirai de trifti ŏ.2c.15.   Item mi trouo effere debito i tutto ducati tanti 2c.tanti a al tale.e tanti al tale 2c.Nominádo li toi creditori a uno a vno.E
fe ui fó no chiar:e çe fra noi.o de fcripti o de inftrumenti nominarli.E dhi.E commo. el di el
luogo per molti cafi poteriéno occorrere in iudicio e for de iudicio 2c.

Vtiliffima erortatione:e falutiferi docuḿéti al bó mercatáre príneti.   ca°.4

Cofi difcorfo có diligéça tutte le cofe che te ruroui imobile e ftabile: cóme e detto a una per una:fe foffer ben diecimilia di che conditiomi e faculta fi fua:e banchi
e impreftiti 2c.tutte albuono ordine cóuiene nominarle in ditto cuétario có tut
ti cótrafegni nomi:e cognomi ρ̃to fia piu poffibile.Per ch al mercatáte nõ poffa
no mai le cofe effere troppo chiare.Per linfiniti cafi che nel trafico poffano occorrere:com
mo ala giornata fa chi in effo fe ererita.E pero bé dia el prouerbio che bifogna piu ponti
a fare vn bó mercatáte. che a fare vn doctore de leggi.Chi e colui che poffa nüerare li pũti:
e cafi che ale mani uengono ali mercatanti.Ora ρ marc.Ora ρ terra.Ora a tempi de pace e
dabondantia.Ora a tempi de guerre e coreftie.Ora a tempi de fanita e morbi.Ne quali te
piè occurréçe li conuiene faper prendere foi partiti.Si ρ li mercati:cómo ρ le fieri che ora i
una patria e cita fi fãno.E ora in laltra 2c.E pero ben fe figura e afimiglia el mercatante al
gallo.Quale e fraglialtri el piu uigilante animale che fia:e diuerno e di ftate fa le fue notur
ne uigilie.che mai per alcũ tempo refta.Auenga che de filomena fe dica:cioe del rofignuo
lo che tutta la nocte canti:non dimeno quefto fi ρ de ftate al caldo tempo ucrificare: ma
non dinuerno:cómo la experienta e impronto adimoftrarlo.E ancho fia fumigliata la fua
tefta a vna che habia céto ochi.che anchora nõ li fóno baftáti:ne in dir ne i fare.Le qual co
fe folole dica chi le pua.Harrinolo.Uentriani.Fiorétini.Benouefi.Napoluani.Milane/
fi.Ancoitá.Breffani.Bergamafchi.Adlani.Senefi Luchefi.Perufini.Urbiati.Forofim
proniani Laghefi.E Ugubini.Caftellani.Borghefi.e Fulignani có Pifali.Bolognefi. e Fe
rarefi.Padouái.Ueróefi.Uigéti.e Padouái.Trani.Lecia.Bari.có Beróta Legl ρ̃u'.rm
laltre i italia del trafico rengano el principato.Oarie la crcella cita de venetia có fiorêça.
Norma e regola dogni partito.chal bifogno aprender fabia.Si che bé dicáo le leggi num
dpali v3. uigilantibus 7 non dormientibus Jura fubueniunt:cioe a chi ueggbia e nó a chi
dorme le leggi fouengáo. E cofi neli diuini officij fi canta da la fancta chiefa.che idio alt vi
gilanti a promeffo la corona. E pero quefto fo el documéto di virgilio dato a Dante:cómo
a fuo fighuolo.Quando nel cáto.: 4°.de lo iferno li dici crortandolo a la fatiga:per laqle
al monte de le uirtu fe peruiene.Ba mai conuen fighiuolo che tu te fpolrri. Diffe el mae-
ftro miо che pur in piuma.In fama nõfi uiene ne fotto coltre. Sotto la qual chi fua uita
cófuma.Cotal ueftigio dffe in terra lafcia. Qual fume i aire e i aqua la fchuma 2c. E vnal
tro vulgar poeta al medefimo ci cóforta dicédo.Non te para ftrania la fatiga ch marte nó
conceffe mai batagl a A quelli che poffando fe nutrica 2c.Lo cremplo anchora del fapiéte
molto fo acio conuéniéte.Dicédo al pigro che fi fpechiaffe nella formicha.E paulo apofto
lo dici che niũ fira degno di corona faluo che chi hara legimamente combattuto 2c.Que
fti recordi li o uoluti adure per tua utilita:acio non te para graue la condiana folicitudine
in tuo facende.marime in tenere la péna in carta:e tutte fcriuere a di per di:qnel che te oc
corre:cómo fe dira nel fcánte.Ma fẽρ fopra tutto p'idio el prio te fia auán gliochi e mai
nõ mancha daludire la meffa la matia Recordádote che ρ lei mai fi pde camio.Ne ρ la o
riça fi fcema riebçe cómo ρ ĝfto fcto uerfo le dici.Nec caritas ορ cf:nec miffa minut uer 2c.
E a ĝftoci erorta el faluatori i fã matheo ĝ̃do dia.Primũ ĝrite regnũ dei:7 hec oia aduce
tur uobis.Cercate rpiani primamẽte el reame ŏ li cieli e poi laltre cofe tépozali e fpãlifacil

mente conſequirete.Pero chel padre voſtro celeſtiale ſa molto bene voſtro biſcanno ʒc̄.E q̄ſto uoglio te ſia baſtāte a tuo amaeſtramēto diuētario ʒc̄.e altri boni vocuſſiti albenfare ʒc̄ De la.:°.parte pricipale vel pſente tractato vitta viſpōne:cōme la ſabia a intendere e in che cōſiſte:circa al trafico:e de li.ʒ.libri pricipali vel corpo mecāteſco. c°.ſ

E quita oza la ſecōda parte pzincipale vel pzeſente tractato laqual vicēmo eſſere la viſpoſilione vi laquale alquāto piu longo cōuie chio ſia:che i laſcedēte a ben chiarirla.E pero vi lei ſaremo voi pri.Luna vitta corpo o uero monte ve tutto el trafico.Laltra vitta corpo o vero monte ve botega.E prima virēmo vel cō po generale ve tutto el manegio le ſue exigēte.Al quale vico prima imediate voppo ſuo fuentario biſognare.ʒ.libzi p piu ſua veſtreça e cōmodita.Luno vitto memoziale.E laltro vetto Giozmale.Laltro veitto.Quaderno.Auēga che molti p le poche loz facende facino ſolo cō li voi ſecōdi:cioe giozmale e quaderno.E pero prima viremo vi luno cioe memoziale.E poi ſuſequētemēte ve lialtri voi velor modi:uerſi e vie cōmo vebiano eſſere tenuti.E prima va remo ſua viſſinitione.

Del primo libzo vitto memoziale o vero ſquartafoglio o vachetta ql che ſenten da e commo in eſſo ſe habia a ſcriuere:e p chi. ca° 6

Ade memoziale o vero ſe condo alcuni vachetta o ſqrtafoglio e vn libzo nel q̄le tutte le facēde ſue el mercatāte piccole e grādi che ama li vegano.a giorno p gioz no e oza p oza iſcriue.Nel q̄le ryfuſamēte ogni coſa vi uedere e cōprare (e altri manegi)ſcriuēdo ſe vichiara nō laſando vn iota El chi.El che.El quādo.El do uc:cō tutte ſue chiarecce:e meticni:cōmo a pieno vi ſopra in lo enuentario te viſſi:ſença piu oltra te le repliche.E i queſto tal libzo molti coſtumano ponere lozo fuētario.Ma p che el puote a molte mani e ochi nō laudo te li mobili e ſtabili ſoi a pieno poze.E queſto li zo ſol ſi fa p la furia e le facēde che ſi feſſe.nel quale veue ſcriuere el Patrone,li Fattori Gar ç ni:le vōne (ſe ſāno) in abſēça lū de laltro.Pero chel grā mercatāte nō terra ſempre fermi li garzoni ne factozi.Ma oza li manda in qua:oza li manda in la:i modo che alcuolte lui cō lozo ſōno fora.Chi a fiere chi a mercati ʒc̄.E ſolo le vōne o altri garzoni reſtano a caſa che foſſe a pena ſāno ſcriuere.Epure lozo p non exuiare li aucutozi conuengano venderce e ſco tere:pagare:e cōprare ſecōdo lozdine che val pzincipale li ſia ipoſto.E lozo ſecōdo lozo po te te ogni coſa vebono ſcriuere i vitto memoziale nominādo ſemplicimēte le monete e peſi che ſāno:e trar ſoze a tutte ſoze ve monette che vendano o cōprano o uero pagano e ſcota no po che i queſto tale non fa caſo a che moneta ſi caui foze.cōmo nel giozmale e quader noich viſotto ſe dira ʒc̄.e quaderniero aſi tra tutto poi lui quādo veli pōne i giozmale.Bicō tornando poi lo pzincipale vede tutte ſue facende e raſſentate ſe li parc alteramēte ʒc̄.E pero e neceſſario vitto libzo a chi ſa aſai facēde.Per che ſerebe fatiga bellegiare:e per ordine ogni coſa la prima uolta mettere i li libzi auctentici e con vligenca tenuti.E i queſto e i tutti al tri prima ponere el ſegno viſoza i ſula copta:acio nel ſucceſſo ve le facēde ſtādo piu o ſeri ptura o uero foznito certo tēpo p la qual coſa tu vozrai vnaltro libzo prēdere.o uero de ne ceſſita te cōuerra quādo queſto foſſe pieno.Ma ale uolte molti coſtumano vuerſe pri: bē che nō ſia pieno anoualmēte far ſoldi:e anche li libzi nuoui cōmo veſotto itēderai.E i vitto ſecondo libzo per vebito ordine biſogna renouare ſegnale viferente val primo:acio vetem po in tēpo ſi poſſa cō preſtecça trouare lozo facēde.Per tal uie ancora milleſimo.E pero be ne ſi coſtuma fra li ueri catolici ſegnare li primi lozo libzi:de quel glozioſo ſegno velq̄l fug gi ogni noſtro ſpiritual nemico:e la caterua tutta inſernal meritamente trema del ſegno: cioe ve la ſancta croci dal q̄ale ancora neli teneri anni a iparar ve legere lalfabeto cōmen çaſti.E poi li ſequēti libzi ſegnarai per ordine velfabeto:cioe ve.A.E poili terçi del.B.ʒc̄. viſcozrendo per ordine vlalfabeto.E chiamaſe poi libzi croci cioe Memoziale croci. Giozmal croci:cioe Quaderno croci:cioe Alfaberō vero extratto croci cioe. ʒc̄. E poi ali ſcoi libzi ſe v̄a Memozial.A.Giozmal.A.Quaderno.A.ʒc̄.E ve tutti queſti li) bzi el numero ve loz carti ſi conuen ſegnare p molti reſpecti e cautele che aloperante ſāin no ve biſogno.Aueuga che molti vichino nel giozmale e memoziale non biſognare: p che le coſe ſe guidano i ſilicate a di p di:vna ſotto laltra che ſia baſtante a loz ritronare. Que ſti tali virebono el uero ſe le facende ve vna giozmata non paſſaſſero vna carta.Ma noi ve dimo che molti groſſi traſicanti non che una carta ma doi e tre nēpirano in vn giozno ve le qual poi (chi violeſſe far male)nepotrebbe tagliare e cauare una.La qual fraude nō ſi po trebe poi per uia vli giozni cognoſcere ne viſcernere.Per che li di ſon quelli che ſēça dubio poffano fucceffiuamente fequirei non dimanco el man camento.fira fatto.Si che per qfto e altri afai refpecti fempre e buono numerare e fignare in tutti li libri mercantefchi.E di ca fa e di botega tutte le carti zc. ca°.7

Del mo como i molti luoghi fe.babio auctenticare tutti li libri mercatefchi e p cb e dachi. Quefti tali libri conuegoli fecondolufance bone de diuerfi paefi:neli quali luo ghi mifo retrouato portarli: e aprefentarli a certo officio de mercarati como fon no confoli nela cita de perofa e a loro narrare como quefti fono li toi libri i ligli tu intendi fcriuere o uero far fcriuere de ma del tale.zc.ogni tua facenda ordina tamente.E dire a cbe monete tu li uoli tenere:cioe a.$.de picioli:o uero a.$.de groffi:o uero a duc.e.$.zc.Q vero a fio.e.f.o.o ro a.6.tari grani.o.zc.Lc ql cofe fepre el real mercatare helpricipio dogni fuo libro deue pore nella p² carta.E qdo mano fe mutaffe nella fcriptu ra valtri cbe nel pricipio fe diceffe:conuenfe p uia del ditto officio chiarirlo.El fcriua poi de tutto cio fa mettoe i regiftri de ditto officio como i tal di m prefentafti tali e tali libri fegna ti del tal fegno zc.E biamato lu cofi e laltro cofi zc.Di qli el tale a tante carti el tale tate zc li quali diffe douere effere tenuti p ma fua o del tale zc.Ma i vno (ditto memoriale.Q ro uacbetta.o fecondo alcuni ditto fquartafacio).ciafcuno di fuoi familiari de cafa e la gior nata poteua fcriuere per le ragioni fopra afegnate.E aloro ditto fcriua de fua propria mano in nome de lofficio fcriuara el medefimo nella prima carga de li tuoi libri:e fara fede ogtut to zc.E boleralli del fegno del ditto officio i fede autentica per tutti li iudici) cbe acadeffe p durli.E quefta tal ufanca merita fumamete effere comedata zc.E cofi li luoghi cbe la obfer uano.pero cbe molti tegano li loro libri dopu.Unoine moftrano al conpratore e laltro al vendiroze.e cbe pegio e fecondo quello. giurano e fpgiurano zc.cbe maliffio fano.E po p tal uia dofficio degno andando:no poffano cofi de facili dir bufcia:ne fraudare el.primo zc Li quali poi con diligenca fegnari e ordinatamente difpofti tu teneuai co lo nome o dio a cafa agomecare a fcriuere tue facede.E prima nel giornale ponere per ordine tutte le puie de lo inuentario nel modo cbe fequente intenderai.Ma prima intendi come nel memoriale fe coftuma dire zc.

Como fe debino dittare le partite i ditto memoriale co erepli ca°.8

Jae ditto fe bene ai amente como i ditto memoriale:o uero uacbetta:o vero fqr tafacio fecondo altri cbe oguuno di tuoili po fcriuere.E pero del dittare tal ptre i effo no fi po dare piena doctrina.pero cbe cbi intedera :e cbi non di toi di ca fa.Ma el comu coftume e quefto cioe.Octamo cbe tu babi coprato alquante pecce de pano(vtpura.20.biandro brefani)p duc.12.luna bafta cbe femplicimete ponga la prita cofi dicedo cioe.Jn quefto di babiamo o uero a o coprato dal felipo de rufoi dabef fapani n°.20.biachi breffai pofti i fu lauolta di 6 ftefao raglia pietra zc.Loga lua o le pecce di coueto br.tati zc.Per duc.tann luna zc.fegnate del tal n° zc.nominado fe fono atre lici o uero a la piana baffio alti fini o mecai bergamafchi o uigetini o verofi padoani fiorutini o matoai zc.E fimiliter nominar fecifoffe fenfale e narrar fel mercato fo a cotati tutto o ro parte cotati e pte termene:e dir quato tepo.Q uero noiar fe foffe pte o cotati e parte robbe E fpecificare cbe robbe.o de numero pefo e mifura.E a cbe pregio el.M°.o etc°: o uero .$. o uero a rafo de conto zc.Q uero fe foffero tutti a tepo e narrare cbe termic.Q de galie o barutto.o de galie de fiadra o de retorni de naui zc.E fpecificare la muta de dirte galie.Q de naui zc. o fe foffe termine de fiere:o altre folenira: como per lafenfa prorima futura zc.o uero p la pafqua denadal zc.o uero de refureri.o uero caricuale zc.piu e maco fedo cbe uoi cocludefte el mercato.E finaliter i ditto memoriale no fi conuerra laffare poto alcu no.E fe poffibile foffe dir quate parolle ue interpofero p cbe (como nel muentario fopra ro detto)al mercante le chiarecce mai foro troppo zc.

De li.9.modi p li quali comunamete fi coftuma fra li mercati coprare ede le mercatie qua li al piu o le noite de neceffita atempo fi comprano. ca°.9

Poi cbe al comprare fiamo nota cbe quello cbe tu compri po acadere comuna men te i.9.modi:cioe a denari.contanti.o uero a termine.o vero al incontro dar robba.Qual certo comunamente editto baratto.o uero a pte o.e parte termie.o vero a parte cotati e parte robbe.o uero a pte robbe.e pte termine. o vero p afe gnatione de ditta.o uero parte i ditta e pte termie a te.o uero pte ditta e parte robba.Jn li qli.9.modi el piu de le uolte fe coftuma comprare.E fe per altro uerfo faceffe in uefita:i ql

modo propjo fa che tu'e gliakri per te nel mcmonale la narm aponto con uerira e farai be
ne ȝc. E cofi quando tu facefti le tue compʒe a tempo. Comino fe coftuma ale volte tarfi de
guari. O vero biade.vini.fali E curanni oabeccari E feȝbi.cbe fi obliga etuenditore.al cópʒa
core.oe oar tutto el guaro cbe per quel tempo bara. E cofi el becaio te uccide e promette tut
ti li cori. pelle.fego.cbe per ȝllo anno in fua beccaria.fara ȝc. La tal foʒa.per tanto la ȝ.ȝc.
E la tale per tanto ȝc. E cofi de li feȝbi oe manȝo.caftroni ȝc. E le pelle motonine nere·p
tanto el c°.acóto. E tanto le montonine blancbe ȝc. E cofi oe liguari. O biade fpecificar con
co el O⁹. E tanto lo ftaro.o el moggio.o la coʒba.oele biade: como inful chiuli oe perolcia
fi coftuma. E oe guari.al Boʒgo falepolcro noftro. Mercatello. Santagnilo. Ciri o caftel
lo. Furli ȝc. Siche oe ponto in ponto. far mentione oi tutto a pieno in oitto memoriale. o
per te:o per altri cbe li fcriua. E narra la cofa femplicemente. como te nafcura ȝc. E oi poi
el bon quaderniei.i capo oe. 4.o.5.o vero.8.giorni. Piu e manco cbe feceffe oel oitto meino
riale metarle in gioʒnale.a di per oi tutte comme le fonno nafcute. Ma folo in quefto oiffe
rente: cbe non bifogna cbe in oitto gioʒnale fe oiftenda con tante filaltocch oe paroile.com
mo fe fatto in oitto memoriale. Pero cbe bafta alui una uolta bauere lacofa ben oigefta in
oitto memoriale. Al qual poi el gioʒnale fempre fa a referire. Pero cbe quelli cbe coftuma
no tenere.ȝ.libri(a modo oitto)mai oebano ponere cofa in gioʒnale.cbe prima non labuino
in oitto memoriale ȝc. E quefto bafti quanto aloʒdine oe oitto memoriale. O per te o p al
tri toi fia tenuto ȝc.   E nota cbe per quanti modi tu oa altri poi compʒare.cofi tu per tan
ti poi vendere. E per confequente altri po comprare oa te. Nel qual vendere non mi ftedo
altra mente. Pero cbe tu per te babiando quefta foʒma oe compaʒare.poʒrai a letarti ȝc.

Del fo libro principale mercantefco.oitto gioʒnale: quel cbel fia e comme fe oebia oifpo
nere ordinatamente.   Capitolo   10

L fo libro ordinario mercantefco.e oitto gioʒnale. Nel quale.(comme e ourò)
oeue effere el medefimo fegno cbe in lomemoʒiale. E carti fegnate ȝc. Comino
oifopra oel memoʒial e ourò. Per le oıte cagioni. E fempre nel principio de ca
duna carta:fe oeue mettere el MaIefimo.e oi. E oipoi oemano in mano ponere
prima le partite tutte oel tuo cuentario. Nel qual gioʒnale.(per effere tuo libro fecreto)poʒ
rai a pieno narrare e oire tutto quello cbe oi mobile e ftabile te ritroui. Referendote fepre
al oitto foglio cbe per te.o per altri foffe fcritto.el quale in ȝlcbe caffa.o fcarola.o filȝo maȝ
ȝo. o tafca : cbe cofi fe ufa el feruarai. Commo te oiro oe le lettere. E fcripture menure. ma
le partite oel oitto gioʒnale:fi conuengono foʒmare e oittarc per altro modo piu liguidoʒ:
non fuperfluo.ne ancbe tropo ouminuto : commo qui feguente oe alquante partite te oaro
exemplo. Ma prima e oanotare el bifogno oi ooi termini.cbe in oitto gioʒnale fi coftuma
ufare.nela cita maxime excella oe Uinegia.Di qualli immediate oireino.

De li.2.termini nel oitto gioʒnale ufati.maxie i Uenegia.Luno oitto. Per. e laltro oit
to. A. e quello cbe per loʒo fe babia a oenotare.   Capitolo. 11.

Oi fonno(commo e oitto)li termini ufirati i ditto gioʒnale.Luno e ditto. Per
E laltro e ditto. A. Liȝli bano loro fignificati.cafcuno feparato. Per lo. Per.
fempre fe oinota el oebitore. o vno o piu cbe fe fieno. E per lo. A. fe oinota lo
creditore.o vno o piu cbe fe fieno. E mai fi mette prita ordinaria i gioʒnale(cbe
al libro grade fabia apoʒre)cbe nó fe oinoti p°. li oidim ooi termini. Deli ȝli fepʒe nel pʒin
cipio de ciafcuna prita fi mette el. Per. Pero cb p°.fi oeue fpecificare eldebitore.e di poi ime
diate elfuo creditore.diuifo lū dalaltro p ooi ȝȝolcrre cofi.II Cómo nclo ex° oifotto te fira
noto ȝc.   Del modo a fap ponere e dittare le pʒite i lo gioʒnale del dare e de lauere có
molti exepli. E deli ooi altri termini nel qderno ufirati luno oetto Caffa.e laltro Caucdale
E quello cbe fi babia intendere.   Capitolo. 12.

Dóca có lonome de oio comeȝarai apócre nel tuo gioʒnale. La p°.pʒita oel tuo
iuétario, cioe la ȝ°.dch ò cótarti:cbe te ritroui. E p iape ponere oitto iuentario
allibʒo.e gioʒnale. bifogna cb tu umagini ooi altri termini.luno oitto. Caffa e lal
tro ditto Caucdale. Per la caffa.fintéde la tua p°.ouero boʒficia. Per locouedale.fe ité de tut
to el tuo móte e coʒpo oe faculta pʒite. E lȝle caucdale.i tutti lupʒincipii oe ȝderni.e gioʒnali
mercátefchi:fepre oeucffere pofto creditore. E la oirra caffa fepre oeueffr pofta debitrice.
e'mai p nullo tpo nel mancȝio mercátefco.lacaffa po cére creditrici.ma folo debitrici ouero
para. Pero cb ȝñ nel bilácio del libro fi trouaffe creditrici oenotarebe errore nel libʒ cómo
di fotto a fuo loco te oaro fūmaria recoʒdanȝa. Ora uel gioʒanale oitta pʒita oe cótranti fi
oeue mettere e dittare in quefto modo. vȝ

Forma õ metter i giornale.   M.cccc°.Lxxxiiii.a dì.8.nouēbre i venegia.   pri°
Per caſſa de cõtanti. A cauedal de mi tale 2c.p cõtanti mi trouo i qlla al priūte.fra oro e mo
nete.arzēto e ramo õ diuerſi cogni.cõe ape i lo fogilo delo iuētario poſto i caſſa. 2c. i tutto
duc.tãri doro.E monete duc.tantiual i tutto almodo nro venitiano.a oro.cioe a groſſi.24
pen duc.e picioli.32.per groſſo a 8.a oro.   2°.   §   ß   ĝ   p
Per gioie ligate e diſligate de piu ſorti: A cauedal ditto. per balaſſi tanti. ligati 2c. peſano
2c.E ſaffiri tanti 2c.e rubini e diamãti 2c.Cõe ape al ſopraditto iuētario.Quali metto ta
lere a comũ corſo.libalaſſi tanto. 2c. E coſi dirai de ciaſcuna ſorta.ſuo pgio cõuno. mon
tano in tutto ducati tanti 2c. vagliano.   §   ß   ĝ   p
E hauēdo tu nominato vnauolta el dì.E ancora el debitore.e ancora el creditore.nõ trame
çandoſe altra prira poi dire. A dì ditto.Per ditto.E al ditto 2c.per piu breuita.
Per argenti lauorati: Al ditto che ſintēde pur el cauedal p piu ſorte argēti cal prite mi trouo
cioe Bacili tanti 2c.E rami tanti 2c.E tacçe tante 2c.E piron tanti 2c.E coſtier tãte 2c.
peſano in tutto tanto 2c.val   §   ß   ĝ   p
Deſtinguēdo.bene di põto p qſte prime prite ogni coſa cõe feſti in lo iuētario. Ponēdoli
tu p te vn comun pgio.E fallo graſſo.piu preſto che magro.cioe Se ti pare che vaglino.
20.e tu dì.24.2c. Acio che meglio te habia reuſcire el guadagno.E coſi de mano in mano
porrai tutte laltre coſe.con ſuoi peſi n°.e valute.2c.   4°.
Per panni de lana de doſſo: Al ditto.p veſte tante di tal colore 2c.E a tal foggia 2c. Fode
rate 2c.vſate o vero noue 2c.a mio doſſo.o vero de la mia dona.o uero de figlioli 2c.Met
to valere a comune ſtima.luna p laltra.in tutto duc tanti 2c.E p mantelli tãti de tal colore
2c.Cõe diceſti ble veſte e coſi dirai de tutti ditti pãni p tutto.   5°.   §   ß   ĝ   p
Per pãni lini: Al ditto p lençoli tanti 2c, E tutto narra comme ſta in lo inuentario, monti
no E vagliano.2c.   6°.   §   ĝ   a
Per letti de piuma: Al ditto 2c.p piume tãte 2c.E qui narra commo ſta in lo inuentario.
montano o vagliano.   7°.   §   ĝ   p
Per cençer mechini: Al ditto.p colli tanti 2c.narra cõmo i inuētario.ſi contene.montano e
vagliano a comune ſtima 2c.duc.tanti 2c.   §   ß   ĝ   p
     E coſi poi tu p te ſteſſo ſeqrai di porre tutte laltre prite de qlaltre robbe.declaſcuna facē
do ſua prita.ſepata.cõmo q õ cçer ſe ditto. Ponēdoli pgio de comũ corſo.commo diſopra
e ditto.Elorn° ſegnte peſi.commo de ponto ſtãno i ditto fogilo diuētario.Chiamādo den
tro laprita.cõ moneta cõ tuvolt.E nel trar fora.conuē poi cõ ſieno a vna ſorta.Perch non
ſtaria bene.a cauar fora.a diuerſe ſorte 2c. E tutte ditte prite õ giornale ſererai a 1°.auna ti
rando la riga.de q°o dura tua ſcriptura. narratiua. fin al termine che ſi tra fora. El mede
ſimo modo ſeruarai ale prite del memoriale 2c.E ſo che tu del memoriale mettarai i giorna
le.coſi a vna a vna.andarai depēnando i lo memoriale.con vna ſola.riga.a trauerſo coſi./.
cõ denotãra qlla tale prita.eēr poſta i lo giornale 2c.E ſe tu non voleſſi trauerſare la pri°.cõ
vna linea.e tu lāciarai.la p°.lfa del principio dela prita.o uero lultia.commo al capo di qſta.
ſatto. O vero farate tu da te qlcõ alt°.ſegno.tale cõ tu itēda.p qllo ditta prira eēr ſtata meſ
ſa igiornale 2c.E auēga cõ tu da te poſſi uſare molti varij e diuerſi termini e ſegni.nõ dime
no te debi ſēpre ſtudiare de vſare licomun.che p li altri trafficãti i tal paeſe ſi coſtuma diſa
re. Acio non para tu ſia diſcrepante daluſitato modo mercatelco 2c.
     Del 3°.evitt°.lib°. principale mercatelco.dette del qderno cõmo deba eēr ſatto e ól ſuo alſa
beto commo ſe debia ordinare. vgnolo e dopio.   Cap°. 13.   E poſte che tu ha
rai ordinatamēte tutte le tuoi prite al giornale.poi biſogna che di qllo.le caui. E poetile in lo
3°.libro ditto qderno grāde.Elql comunamēteſi coſtuma fare de doi tãte carti chel giorna
le. In ſoqle conuerra eēr vno Alfabeto.overo Reptorio ovoi dir Trouarello ſo alcuni. ala
fioxētina dicti lo ſtratto. Nel ql porrai tutti debitori e creditori. Per le lfe che comēçano
con lo n°.dele ſue carti.cioe quelli che comēçã p.a. i.a.2c. E del dopio alfabeto.E qsto
ſimilmēte commo ſopra dicēmo conuē cõ ſia ſegnato el medemo ſegno chl giornale e me
moriale.Poſtoui el n°.dele ſue carti. E diſopra i margine. da luna bãda e laltra. el mileſimo
E in la prima. ſua carta.dentro porrai debitrici la caſſa. ſi commo ella e la p°. del giornale.
coſi deue eēr p°.nel qderno. E tutta qlla ſaciata.ſi coſtuma lafaria ſtare per dieta caſſa.E in
dar ne i bauere non ſi pone altro.E qſto p che la caſſa ſe manegia piu che prita di ſio.a ora
p ora.i metter e cauar dinari. E po lſe laſſa el cãpo largo. E qſto qderno cõuē che ſia riga
gato.de tãte righe.õte che ſorte monete volitrar ſore. Se trarai. § ß õ p. Farai.4.righe.
e dinãçe ale §.ſarane vnaltra.p metarui el n°.dele carti de le prite che iſueni de dare. E ba

uere ſe icatenano. E vináče farai.2.righe. p potere metterc. li ot ô mano i mano. commo ne
li altri qderni bai viſto che piu non miſtédo i qſto ꝛc.p poter trouar pſto lepꝛite ꝛc. E pur
ſira ſegnato croci commo li altri.
Del modo a poꝛtar le pꝛite de gioꝛnale in quaderno. e pche de una in gioꝛnale ſene facia
voi in quaderno: e del modo a depennare le pꝛite in gioꝛnale e de li voi numeri dele carti
del quaderno che in le ſue margine ſi pone e pche.   Cap°   14.

Er laqual coſa.ſappi che oi tutte le pꝛite che tu barai poſte in logioꝛnale, al qua
derno gráde.te ne cōué ſepꝛe fare voi.cioe vna in dare e laltra in bauere pche liſi
chiama debitoꝛe p lo. Per. E lo creditoꝛe p lo. A. cómo oiſopꝛa oicémo ch ô
luno e de laltro.ſi deue da pſe fare 1ª.pꝛita: qlla del debitoꝛe. ponere ala man ſinī
ſtra. E qlla del creditoꝛe.ala man oextra. E in qlla del debitoꝛe.chiamare lacarta. doue ſia
qlla del ſuo'creditoꝛe. E coſi'in qlla del creditoꝛe.chiamare la carta oi qlla doue ſia. El ſuo
debitoꝛe. E in qſto modo ſepꝛe uégano incattenate tutte le pꝛite del oitto qderno gráde. nel
ql mai ſi deue metture coſa in dare che qlla ancoꝛa non ſi ponga in baueꝛe. E coſi mai ſi deue mettere coſa in bauere che ancoꝛa. qlla medeſima cō ſuo amōtare nō ſi metta in dare. E
oi qua naſcſ poi.albilancio che del lib°.ſi fa.nel ſuo ſaldo táto cóuié che ſia el dare.qꝛto laue
re. Cioe ſūmate tutte le pꝛite che ſiráno poſte in dare ſe foſſero bene. 10000. va pꝛe in ſu vn
foglio. E oi poi ſūmate ſimilmēte tutte qlle che in bauere ſi trouano. tanto debbe fare luna
ſumma qꝛto laltra.altramēte demoſtrarebbe eére errore nel oitto qderno.cóe nel modo del
far ſuo bilancio ſe oira a pieno ꝛc. E coſi cóe ouina de gioꝛnale ne fai.2. al qderno. coſi a qlla
pꝛita che del gioꝛnale leui farai voi righe a trauerſo ſo dôvai leuando. cioe ſe p².tu la metti i
dare. Pꝛia farai 1ª.riga atrauerſo. verſo al prin°.dela pꝛita.che oinota eér poſta in dare al q
derno. E ſe la metti in bauere. o pꝛima.o poi cóe acade ale uolte fare al qdernieri qdo li aca
de ſcriuere i luogo.ch li in qlla carta li nandera.2.o.3. p nō ui bauere a toꝛnare.ſene ſpaça oi
metterle li aloꝛa. E po fo che mette coſi deue depennare p bauerla meſſa in bauere. farai tal
tra depēnatura.verſo man oextra. dal canto doue fineſci la pꝛita che ōnotara eér meſſa i ba
uere. leql linee ſtaranno cóe oiſopꝛa in qſto uedi figurato a lapꝛita. p².dela caſſa. luna oitta
linea. de dare. e lalt².de bauere. E coſi oalato i margine oinanç alpꝛincipio biſogna che pō
gbi.2.nuᶤ.luno ſotto laltro.ql oi ſopꝛa che denoti la pꝛita.del debitoꝛe.a qꝛte carti che la ſia
poſta in lo qderno E qllo de ſotto che denoti le carti de oitto qderno. doue ſia poſto el cre-
ditoꝛ.cóe vedi li ala pꝛita dela caſſa oiſopꝛa i qſto.che ſta coſi.!. ſeça tramecço. E ancoꝛa al
cuni coſtumano coſi cō tramecço. ;. a guiſa de rotti.che nō fa caſo. Ma e piu bello ſença tra
mecço. Aoio adxi vede nō pareſſero ſpecçati. O vero rotti ꝛc. E vol oire qllo. 1°. oi ſopꝛa che
la caſſa. E nella p².carta del qderno. E cauedale. E nella fa carta de oitto qderno.i bauere.
e qlla in dare ꝛc. E nota che ſepꝛe qꝛto piu pſſo tu poꝛai mettere clcreditoꝛe al ſuo oebitoꝛe.
ſera piu liçadro. auéga che poſto doue ſiuoglia tanto móti. Ma p riſpetto del mileſimo.che
ale uolte ſe iterpōe fra 1ª.pꝛiª.e lalt². reſpōde male. E cō fatiga.nō poca.ſe ritrouano loꝛ tpi
cóe ſa chi .pua ch ogni coſa coſi a pieno nō ſi po oire. Ma bũo².ch áncoꝛa tu alqꝛto cō tuo na
turale ingegno ta iuti. E po ſepꝛe ſtudia oaſettar ditto creditore immediate a pſſo el ſuo de
bitoꝛe in la medema faciata.o vero ila iuediate ſeqnte.nō interponédoui fra luno e laltro.al
tra pꝛita. Perocbe nel.ppꝛio gioꝛno che naſci eldebitoꝛe in qllo medemo naſci el creditoꝛe
E p qſto riſpetto ſepꝛe ſe deue acoſtar luno a lalt° ꝛc.
Del modo a ſape dittare le pꝛite de lacaſſa e cauedale nel quaderno in dare e baueꝛe: e ōl
mileſimo che oiſopꝛa nel pꝛincipio dela carta a lanti co ſi mette in eſſo: e dela ſua mutatione
e del cōptir liſpacij dele carti fo le pꝛite piccole e grádi fo elbiſogno dele facéde.   Cap°. 15.

Oꝛ qſte coſe diſcoꝛſe.a tuo amaeſtramēto.oꝛmai ditamo la p².pꝛita de la coſa i
dare e poi qlla del cauedal in bauere in lo libꝛo gráde. Ma cóc e oitto p². deſo
pꝛa nel quaderno pꝛincipal el mileſimo alabacco antico. cioe per alfabeto coſi.
M cccc. Lxxxriii. ꝛc.El di nō ſe coſtuma mettarlo oiſopꝛa in loquaderno cóe in
lo gioꝛnale.pche 1ª.pꝛita in quaderno.bara diuerſi di. E po nō ſi poꝛra ſeruar oꝛdine deli
di.diſopꝛa cóe apieno nel ſeqnte cap°.ſe dira. Ma dētro dela pꝛita cóe intédcrai la p².uolta
E poi coſi dalato in lo ſpacio che diſopꝛa dicémo dinançe ala pꝛita. qdo tal partita naſceſſe
daltro mileſimo che diſopꝛa nel pꝛincipio dela carta foſſe ſcritto che ſole auenire acbi de an
no in anno nō ꝛipoꝛta e ſalda ſuoilibri ſiche tal mileſimo ſi poꝛra difuora.nndo in margine
ꝛipetto a pōto a qlla pꝛita li nata cōe uedi poſto qui diſotto. qſto ſolo auene in lib° gráde
che in li altri nō po auenire. Dóca ꝛíaai coſi.tꝛaédola fore pure alabacco ãtico p piu belleça

non ꝟimeno aqual che tu te caui non fa caſo ꝛc. Donca ꝟirai coſi.

yꝭs.   M.cccc Lxxxiiij.

Caſſa ꝟe cõtanti ꝟie ꝟare a ꝟi.8.nouẽbꝛe.per cauedal per contanti ꝟe piu ſoꝛte fra oꝛo e mo
nete me trouo bauere in quella in queſto pꝛeſente ꝟi in tutto ca.2.   8. r͂m.ꝧ ꝗ ꝑ

E qui nõ biſogna che troppo te ſtẽda.p bauer bẽ gia iſteſo in gioꝛnale. Ma ſempꝛe ſtudia
ꝟir bꝛeue.La pꝛima nel comẽçare ſe ꝟici alquanto:ale ſequẽti in la medema ſol ſe ꝟici.e a
ꝟi ꝟitto ꝛc.per lo tale. car.   8   ꝧ ꝗ ꝑ
L aqual coſi poſta che lbarai.ꝟepẽnarai in gioꝛnale in ꝟare comme ſopꝛa te ꝟiffi.E poi i ba
uer per lo cauedal ꝟirai coſi.v3.

yꝭs   M.cccc°.Lxxxiiij.

Cauedal ꝟe mi tale ꝛc. ꝟie bauere a ꝟi.8.nouẽbꝛe.per caſſa.per contanti me trouo in quel
la fin al ꝟi preſente in oꝛi e monete ꝟe piu ſoꝛte in tutto. car. 1.   8.r͂m.ꝧ o g o ꝑ o

E coſi ancoꝛa.i ꝗſta baſta ſucciniamẽte ꝟire per lacagion ſopꝛa ꝟitta.ꞁaltre poi che ꝗ ſotto
ala medema pꝛita.ſe baueranno apoꝛꝛe fin che la ſia piena baſtara adire.E a ꝟi tanti ꝛc.per
ſatal coſa ꝛc.Cõe uedi acẽnato qui ꝟa canto. e anco in fin ꝟi ꝗſto barai exemplo. coſi ſequi
rai con bꝛeuita in tutte.maxime in quelle parate che a te ſolo aſpettano.cioe che non bai a
rendere conto adalcuno. Ma in ꝗlle che tu bauerai a rendere cõto adaltri.alꝗto piu ti cõ
uerra ꝟire.auenga che ſempꝛe ſe recoꝛre.per le chiaregge al gioꝛnale ꝛc.E poi ꝟarai laltra ꝟe
pẽnatura.a ꝗlla ꝟel gioꝛnale in bauere.cõe ſopꝛa ti ꝟiffi in.12°.cap° E in lamargine ꝟauan
ti.ala pꝛita.poꝛrai li ꝟoi numeri cõe ꝟiffi pur in ꝟitto loco ꝟele carti ꝟoue ſõno. El debitoꝛe
el creditoꝛe.cioe ꝗllo ꝟel ꝟebitoꝛe ꝟeſopꝛa.E ꝗllo ꝟel creditoꝛe ꝟe ſotto cõe facemo ꝟiſopꝛa.
ala pꝛita ꝟe lacaſſa. E poi ſubito poꝛrai in lo tuo alfabeto.cioe repꝛtoꝛio. ꝗſto ꝟebitoꝛe e credi
toꝛe.ognuno ala ſua lꞁa cõe ſai che ꝟiſopꝛa ꝟiffi.Cioe la caſſa al la lꞁa. C. ꝟicẽdo ꝟetro in ꝗ
ſto modo.cioe.Caſſa ꝟe cõtanti. K. 1.   E ancoꝛa el cauedal poꝛrai al. C. ꝟicendo. Ca
uedal ꝟe mi ppꝛio. K. 2.   E coſi p tuo ingegno aꝟarai aꝇmando. tutte le pꝛite. c li nõl
ꝟe li ꝟebitoꝛi perſõe e robbe ꝛc.E coſi ꝟe creditoꝛi.poꝛrai nel ꝟitto repertoꝛio. a leſue lettere
acio poi con facilita poſſi ſubito retrouarli in ꝟitto quaderno grande ꝛ cetera.

E nota che bauendo tu pꝟuto el tuo ꝗderno p alcun caſo ꝟerobaꝛia.o incẽdio ꝟi foco.o
naufꝛagii ꝛc.E bauẽdo tu luno ꝟe li altri ꝟoi libꝛi.Cioe memoꝛiale.o vero gioꝛnale. cõ eſſo
poꝛrai ſempꝛe refare vnaltro ꝗderno.cõ le medeſime pꝛite a ꝟi p ꝟi. E ponerle al numeꝛo ꝟe
le medeſime che i ꝗl pꝛo ſi retrouauano.Maxime bauẽdo tu el gioꝛnale.ꝟoue ꝗ̃do ne leua
ſti le pꝛite.E põeſti al lꞁb°.tu imargie poneſtiꞁli ꝟoi nui.ꝟli ꝟebitoꝛi e creditoꝛi.ꞁuo ſoura ꞁal
tro che chiamauano le carti. ꝟel ꝗderno doueranoſituati.e ꝟipoto atante carti li poꝛrai fa
re ritoꝛnar cõ tuo ingegno ꝛc.E ꝗſto baſti ꝗ̃to a vna pꝛita poſta ꝛc.   Poi la ſa pꝛita chꝟ
ſo ꝟele çoſe al ꝗderno ponẽdola a ſuocõꝟecẽte luogo ꝟittarai coſi.E pꝛiª. ſempꝛe ſença piu
te replichi .poꝛrai ꝟiſopꝛa nel principio ꝟela carta.el milleſimo ſe nõui foſſe poſto p altra pꝛi
ta.p³.poꝛche ale uolte in vna medema facia el quaderniꝛi aſettara.2.o.3.pꝛite ꝧo che cogno
ſcera lo ſpatio eẽr baſtate al manegio ꝟi ꝗlla. pꝟche foꝛſe uedara ꝗlla tale pꝛita bauerſi chia
re ſiade adoperar.E p ꝗſto li ꝟara vn luoco piu anguſto. che a quelle che ſpeſſo li acade. a
dopare:ala giomata cõc ꝟi ſopꝛa.al cap° 13°. de la caſſa e cauedal ſo ꝟetto ꝗl ſi coſtumaua
laſarli tutta laſaciara ꝟel lꞁb°. pꝟche ſpeſſiſſime ſiade.p cẽre gꝛaꝟi le facẽde ſi conuẽgano ma
negiare. E ꝗſto ſol ſi fa p nõ bauer tãto ſpeſſo a far repoꝛio inãçe ꝛc.oꝛa al ppoſito trouato
li el loco cõe ſe ꝟici.ꝟirai coſi in dare.cioe verſo mã ſiniſtra.coſi ſempꝛe ſa apoꝛre el debito.
Cioe ꝟe piu ſoꝛte.dienno dare a ꝟi.8. nouẽbꝛe. p cauedale.p pecçi n° tanti ꝛc. peſano tanto
ꝛc.dequali tanti ſonno balaſſi legati ꝛc.E tanti ſaſili ꝛc. E tãti rubini coculegni ꝛc. E tanti
ꝟiamanti creçi ꝛc.lequali in tutto.o vero a ſoꝛta per ſoꝛta metto valere a comun pꝛgio.ꝟe cõ
tanti ꝟuc̃.tanti ꝛc.val car. 2   § 40.ꝧ o.g.o.ꝑ o.

E coſi ꝟepennerai.la pꝛita in gioꝛnale.nel dare tirando la linea comme ꝟe ſopꝛa al.12° cap
te ꝟiffi.E poi andarai al cauedal.E poꝛrai ꝗſta medema con mãco parolle per leragion gia
ꝟiſopꝛa aꝟutte in queſto capitolo e poꝛrꞁa in bauere ſotto quella p³.cꝭꝛgia li bai poſto ꝟela
caſſa. E ꝟirai coſi.v3.

a ꝟi   o   ꝟetto.per çoie ꝟe piu ſoꝛte commo li apare ꝛc. car.3.   §.40.ꝧ o.g.o.ꝑ o.

E coſi poſta farai laltra ꝟepẽnatura.al gioꝛnale i bauer.cõe te mõſtrai ꝟiſopꝛa al.12°.caª.
E poꝛrai i margine li numeri ꝟle carti. ꝟoue tal pꝛire al quaderno poneſti cõmo ꝟicemmo
vno ſopꝛaꞁaltro.comme qui ꝟenãçe apare che metto babi poſta la pꝛita in dar a carti.3.E
ꝗlla ꝟel cauedal ſta pure alogo ſuo a carti.2.pſin tanto chella non e piena.che ꝟipoi innãge

126

a tutte laltre la poztarai.cōmé oifotto ne repozti intēderai apieno.E q̃fto p q̃fta.e a fue fumi lte na baftāte rc̄.E pofta che larai al oitto q̃derno. E afettata in giozmale.e tu fubito lapor̄ rai al reptorio o vero alfabeto.cōe oifopza i q̃fto cap.° fo oetto. Cioe ala fua lfa. B.o vero. 3. fo.pzixe lfa la .pferirai.cōe idiuerfi pacfi acade.che qui i uinegia molto fi coftuma pone/ re el. 3. ooue noi in tofcana ponemo el g.ficbe acordarala tu a tuo Judicio rc̄.

Cōe fe oebino oittare leptite oelemercantie che per inuentario o altro modo lbomo fe ri troua:nel quaderno'in oare e in bauere.   Cap°. 16°.

E altre.4.ptite poi fu fequēti oel tuo mobile.cioe argēti.pāni.lini.letti oe piuma E vefte oe oofto rc̄.Poi p te fteffo facil mēte mettarai oel iuētario in giozmale oe pōto cōe li le ponefti.oenotate.pche cōe oicēmo oifopza cap°.6? q̃fto tal inuenta rio nō fi caua oel memoziale.p la ragiōe li afegnata.E po fuo oittare in giozmale E ancoza nel grā lib.° i oare e bauere.e oi pozze alalfabeto.lafciaro oz mai fedre al tuo pegri no ingegno oel q̃l molto me cōfido E folo la. 7ª. prita oe çeçer mechini che ti troui afettrare mo igiozmale.E ancoza al q̃derno laq̃l te fia baftāte e fufficiēte amaeftrainēto a tutte le altre che oimercātia alcun̄. ritrouafte.bauēdo fēpze tu oa te ināçe gliochi loz n°.pefi.e mifure e valute i tutti li modi che tal mercātie fe coftumaffe vēdere.e cōpzare fra mercāti i rialto o fo/ ra.fo lipaefi.oele q̃li cofe q̃ apieno nō e poffibile ponere crēpli.ma cō facilita. oa d̃fti pochi q̃ cōpēdiofamēte pofti poznai oi q̃lūcaltri ipzēdere a tua fufficiēça.po che fe noi volēmo oar te crēplo oel modo verfo e via.oi mercare atranti.lecia.bari.E bctōta.cioe aloz noini ōpefilo ro.E mifure loz rc̄.E cofi oela marca.E anche oela nfa tofcana.troppo ferebbe grāde el volume.che cō breuita· itendo concludere E p q̃lla. 7ª. oe çeçer nel giozmale. oirē cofi. rz. Per çençeri mechini i mōte a refufo.o i colli oirai cōe a te pare rc̄. Al oitto che fintēde caue dal.pche li oifopza imediate larai p ordiñe oe oitto iuētario.cōc oicēmo oifopza cap°. 12°. in la prita fa oe le çoie. p colli tanti pefano. rc̄. E p. g.tante q̃do foffero arefuffo i mōte rc̄. q̃li me retrouo bauere in lemani al di priñte metto oi comū cozfo valere el c°.o vero la g.rc̄. ouc̄.tanti rc̄.mōtano in tutto nettí ouc̄.tanti rc̄. val   g   ß   g̃   p̃

E cofi pofta cō larai nel giozmale. E tu al memoziale.o vero inuētario.la oipena.e lāca.al modo oitto fop°.al.12°.cap° rc̄.E cofi obfuarai p tutte lalt°.rc̄.Di d̃fta cōe fo oetto e oe q̃lū che altra che i giozmale fi metta.fēpre al gran lib°.fi fanno ooppie.cioe 1ª.i oare.e laltra i ba uere cōe oifopza oicēmo c°p.14°.La qual poi nel quaderno in oare.ponendola oittarala i q̃fto modo.Pofto p².fēpze el millefimo fe nō ui foffe in capo oe la carta.feça mettarui el gloz no oifopza po che cōe oicēmo oifopza cap.15? El ri nō fi coftuma pozre fopza nel prin° oe lacarta oel quaderno p rifpetto che in q̃lla medefima facia potrebono eēre piu prite õ oiuer fi oebitozi e creditozi.lequali bēche lenafchino fottoyn milefimo.Cna firanno in oiuerfi me fi e corni.cōe oifcorrēdo p tutto poi apzendere.E q̃do bene ancoza in oitta facia oel libzo grande nō vi foffe altro che 1ª.fola prita oi caffa. o oaltro ancoza el çozno pofto oifopza nel quaderno.nō fipotrebbe feruare.pche in oitta prita.ocozira oi mettere cafi ocozfi in oiuerfi mefi.E oi e p q̃fto e che li antichi oifopza nel quaderno nō bano i libri mercātelchi ufitato mettere el giozno.pche non bano ueduto verfo ne via ne modo che con uerita fi poffa afet tarcilo rc̄.Laqual parrita in oare cofi poznai oicēdo rc̄.

Çençeri mechini.in monte.o uero colli rc̄.oien oare a oi.8.nonembze per cauedal.per colli tanti rc̄.pefano. g.tante rc̄.quali mi trouo bauere in cafa. o uero magaçen al prefente qual oe comun cozfo ftimo valere el cento rc̄.ouc̄.tanti rc̄.E per tutti monta ouc̄. g. p̃. rc̄.val carti. 1.   g   ß   g̃·   p̃.

E cofi oepennarai la partita oel çozmale in oare.cioe a man feneftra cōme piu uolte te oit to E poi in bauere afettarala in q̃fto modo al cauedal comme te monftrai ponere quella oele çoie fopza a cap°.15? cofi rz.

a oi o oetto.per çençeri mechini in monte o vero colli rc̄.car. 3.   g   ß   g̃·   p̃.

E cofi pofta che lbarai oepennarai la partita oel giozmale in bauere.'cioe verfo mande/ ftra.cōe oinançe vedi fatto.E poni li numeri oele carti oināçe alei i margine vno fopza lal tro.Cioe el.3.oifopza oi.2.oifotto pche tu bai meffo el oebitoze a carti.3.nel quaderno. el cre ditoze a.2.Cioe el capital.e fubito poi la metti in alfabeto.o vero reptorio ala fua lfa. Cioe al.3.fe p.3.la cōpiñ.o vero al.B.p la rafo oitta in lo pcedēte ca°.a q̃lla prita fa oele çoie rc̄. Del modo a tenere conto con li offitii publici:e perche:e oe lacamera oelimprefti in ve / netia che fe gouerna per via oe feftieri.   Cap: 17?

                                                                              p̃ iũ

Ora de laltre nõ te ne do.altra norma.cioe di qͤlla de pellami.dafodre cõǧe e cru
de.e fine ꝝc.dele qualia 1°.p 1ª.formarai la prita in giornale e quaderno p ordie
depenando.e ſegnando in tutti li lochi che non teſcordi perche al mercante bi
ſogna altro ceruello.che de beccaria ꝝc. Quella dela camera dipreſti o dal
tro mõte cõe in firença.elmõte dele dote i genoa li lochi o uero altri officii che ſi foſſero cõ
liquali tu baueſſe a fare.per alcuna cagione fa che ſempre con loro tu habia buono ſcõtro.
de dare e de hauere in tutti li modi con qualche chiareçça ſe poſſibile e de man deli ſcriuani
di qͤlli luochi qͤl tiͤ ſotto bona cuſtodia al modo che dele ſcritture e lettere te diro.pͨbe a ǧ
ſti tali officii ſpeſſo ſe ſogliano mutare ſcriuani. liqͤli ognuno a ſua fantaſia uole guidare lili
bri delo officio.biaſimãdo ſempre li ſcriuan paſſati. che non tenuan bon ordine ꝝc. E ſem
pre ognuno pſuade elſuo ordine migliore deli altri.imodo che ale volte inꝏdiano le prite.
de tali officii.che non ſene tien 1ª.cõ laltra. Egual chi cõtali a afare. E po fa che ſia a caſa. E
col eapo aborega.cõ qͤſti tali. E certamͤte forſi el fão a bon fine nõ dimeno moſtrão igno
rãça. E coſi tirrai cõto.cõ li gabellari.e dariari de robbe che tu uͤdi e cõpri.caui e metti nele
terre ꝝc. Cõe ſi coſtuma fare in vinegia.che ſi tiene p li piu dela terra.cõto lõgo cõ lo officio
dela meſſetaria.chi a.2.p.c° e chi a 1ª.p c°. E chi a.4.p c°.ꝝc. Chiamando el libro. del ſen
ſaro.che viſinterpone. e notare al tuo libro. E anche la mare.in ſu ǧ fa. cioc el lib? doue da
in nota li mercati al ditto officio che coſi lo chiamano in veneria po che ciaſcuno ſenſaro a
vno libro.o uero luogo in qualche libro al ditto officio doue lui va a dare in nota li mercati
che fa.ſi cõterrieri.cõe foreſtieri altramͤte caçano in pena.ſaltramͤte faceſſaro. E ſonno prͤ
nati. E bene qͤlla ercelſa.S. licaſtiga e loro.e ſcriuani eb mal ſi portaſcro cõe de molti me ri
cordo.gia neli tͤpi paſſati eͤre puniti ſtraniamͤte. E po ſantamͤte fanno a conſtituirevno
elqͤle a ſolo qͤſta cura.in reuedere tutti lioffici.cioe ſe liloro libᶦ.ſono bñ.oꝶo male tenuti ꝝc.

Comme ſe debia tener conto con lo officio dela meſſetaria in veneria e del ditrare le ſue
partite in memoriale.ꝛornale. e quaderno. e ancora deli impreſti.   Cap°. 18.

E che qͤdo vorai cõ tali offitii tener conto.la camera deimpreſtiti.farai debitrici
de tutta laſorte de cauedali a tanto el c°.ꝝc. Moiando li ſeſtieri doue ſon poſti. E
ſimilmente ſe piu aſa giornata.necõpraſſe che molti ſe ne vendano p te o p altri
cõe ſa chi realto vſa. Nota bñ inchi ſono ſcritti e luoghi .ꝝc. E coſi nel ſcotere li
loro .p.ſepre farala creditrice.a di p di. E ſeſtier p ſeſtieri ꝝc. E coſi cõloffitio dela meſſetaria
El cõto tirrai i qͤſto modo.cioe qͤdo tu comprarai alcuna mercantia p meçço õ ſeſari.alora
de tutto lo amõtare.a raſone de.2.o de.3.o de.4.ꝝc.p c°.ſarane creditore elditto officio dela
meſſetaria. E debitrici qͤlla tale mercantia.plaqͤl cagione tu paghi ꝝc. E po conuene chel cõ
pratore ſempre ritͤga al ueditore nel pagamͤto.de contanti.o vero p altro modo che habia
aſatiſfare non fa caſo.pͨbel ditto officio.non vol andar cercando altro ſenon larata che li
aſpetta.auenga che liſenſari reportino el mercato in nota.cõmo.e cb.e cho.leſtato fatto. per
chiareçce euidͤte de contraͤti qͤdo fra loro.naſceſſe differença alcuna cõe açade. El comun
puerbio dici.chi nõ fa non failla.e chi non failla non impara ꝝc.deleqͤli vͤe volendoſe le prͤi
chiarire hano regreſſo alpercato notaro. plo ſenſaro.al quale ſo li decreti publici li ſi prͤta
fede cõe a publico inſtrumento denotaro. E ſo la forma di qͤllo . di piu dele volte. El degno
offitio deconſoli demercanti.formano le loro furidiche ſentençe ꝝc. Dico adonca compran
do tu alcuna robba.tu dic ſape.qͤllo che la paga de ſñ. E p lamita retieni.al uenditore. Cioe
ſe la robba paga.4.p c°.a qͤllo officio p õcreto.publico del dominio. E tu alui retieni.2. p c°.
E tanto manco lͤconta. E hara el ſuo douere. E tu poi del tutto reſti obligato al ditto offi
tio. E del tutto larai afar creditore al tuo libro contãdo cõlui. E qͤlla tal mercantia farai obi
trici.cõe dicͤmo ꝝc.pͨbe el ditto offitio non vol cercare.chi vende.ma chi compra. E po poi
a tal cõpratori li e conceſſo.di cauare tanto di qͤlla mercantia.p qͤto a pagato la ſñ. foza õ
la terra.in loro bolette.ala tauola.de luſcita.o per mare o p terra che la uogliono cauare ala
giornata. E po conuͤgano li mercanti tenere ben conto con lo ditto officio. acio ſempre ſa
pino qͤto poſſino cauare.pͨbe non ſi laſſano cauar.per piu che ſi cõprino ſe di nouo non
paghino la ſñ.de contani ꝝc.delequali compre ǧ ſequente ti pongo erͤplo. e coſi.del ditto
officio.comme ſe habino a ditrare in giornale. E anche in libro grande. E diro coſi.   Prͤi
ma.in memoriale.ſemplicimente. Jo o vero noi in queſto di poſto diſopra o comprato da ß
ǧuan antonio da meſſina.ꝛucari palermini caſſi n°.tante.pani n°.tanti.peſano in tutto. netti.
de panelle.caſſi.corde.e paglie. ß tante per duc. tãri. el c°.montano duc. tãti ꝝc.abatto per la
ſua parte dela ſñ.a ragion de tanto per c°.duc.ſ.ꝟ.tanti ꝝc.lenſaro ß ǧuan de gagliardi.vale
netti ducati.ꝛ.ꝟ.tanti ꝝc.pagammo contanti.

La medeſima in giornale vira coſi   acontanti.
Per cucari vepalermo. A caſſa contati a f cuan ve antonio vameſina.per caſſi n°.tante pani
n° tanti. peſano netti.ve caſſi.panelle. corde.e paglie. §.tante.a vuc.tanti el c° mótano vuc.
tanti zc.abatto.p la ſua parte vela m̃.a raſon ve tanti per c°. zc. vuc.tanti zc. reſtanonetti.
vuc.tanti zc. ſenſar f.quan ve gaiardi.   §   f   g   p̃

La medeſima in quaderno vira coſi.
Zucari ve palermo.vie vare.adi tale.p caſſa contati a f quan vantonio ve meſina. per panni
numero tanti peſano netti.§.tante per vuc.tanti el cento.montano netti in tutto a carti 1°.
E farai creditrici lacaſſa vi quel tanto zc.   §   f   g   p̃

E ſempre farai loffitio vela m̃.creditore del voppio che tu retenefti aluediroie. cioe p la
ſua e platua pte. zc. E ſepre ſubito notaro la robba imediate i vnalt°.prita ſotto farai credi
toie vitto officio per vitto cucaro cõe harai viſotto.E vibitrici vitta robba. Per erempio vu
na pagata a contanti.Or prendine vna pte a cõtanti e parte. a tpo p°.imemoriale coſi virai.
A contanti e tempo.a di tanti zc.
Jo o comprato a di vetto.Da f quan vantonio.vameſina. cucari ve palermo pani n°. tanti.
peſano netti. §.tante.per vuc.tanti el c°.montano vuc.tanti.abatto per ſua parte ve m̃.a raſo
ve tanti per c°.vuc.tanti zc.ve quali al preſente.li no contati vuc. tari p parte e vel reſto mi
fa tpo fin tutto agoſto .pri°.che vien zc. ſenſar f quan ve gaiardi v.al.   vuc.   g   p̃
E ſappi che ve qlle coſe che ſe ſcriue mercato per loſenſaro.a loffitio non biſogna far ſcrit
to ve man perche el mercato baſta.ma pure a cautela ale uolte ſi fa zc.
Jn giornale la medema vira coſi. prima quel tal ve tutto creditore.E poi vebitore ve ql
la parte ve ð. che lui haue.

yBs.   1 49?.a vi tanti vel tal meſe zc.
Per cucari palermini: A f quan vantonio ve meſina per pani numero tanti peſano netti in
tutto §.tante.a vuc.tanti el c°. montano vuc.tanti zc.abatto per la ſua ptc ve meſſetaria a ra
ſon ve tanti per c°.vuc.tanti zc.reſta netto vuc.tanti zc.ve quali alpreſente li nedebo contar
tanti zc. E vel reſto. mi fa termine fin tutto agoſto proximo che vien. ſenſaro ſer quan ve
gaiardi.val.   §   f   g   p̃

Fanne creditore ſubito loffitio vela m̃.vela ſua rata.
Per li vitti:a loffitio vela m̃.per lamontar ſoura vitto.cioe ve vuc.tari zc a raſo ve tari p c°.
p lamia parte e qlla vel vebitore i tutto monta vuc.g.p.tanti val.   §   f   g   p̃

La parte ve contanti. vebitor lui.E creditore la caſſa. coſi.
Per f quan vatonio.ve miſina: A caſſa cõtati alui p pre peli ſoura vitti cucari fo laforma ðl
mercato.vuc.tari zc.ape vel receuere ſcritto ve ſua mano val.   §   f   g   p̃

La medema in quaderno vira coſi.
Zucari ve palermo.vien dare a vi tal vinouembre . per f quan vantonio vameſina. per pani
n°.tari peſano netti § tante zc.p duc.tanti el c°.mótano netti ve m̃. k.4.   §   f   g   p̃
Quando uoleſſe farne partita nuoua.Ma uolendo ſequitare la prepoſta baſtaua vire a vi.
tanti zc.per f quan vant°.vameſina p pani n°.tari peſano §.tate zc.móta.k.4.§   f   g   p̃

La medemia in hauere vira coſi.
Ser quan vatonio vemeſina.vie hauere a di tanti ve nouembre.per cucari ve palermo. pa
ni n°.tanti peſan netti §.tante per duc.tanti el c°.montano. netti ve m̃.duc.tanti.de quali al
preſente li ne vebio dar contanti duc.tanti zc.delauanço.mi fa tpo per tutto agoſto .prio fu
turo.ſenſar f quan de gagliardi.val   k.4.   §   f   g   p̃

Jn dare lamedema. Per la parte deli contanti.dira coſi.
Ser quan alincontro.die dare a di.tale zc.p caſſa. cõtati alui p pte de cucari.hebi dalui fo
nſi patti duc.tanti zc.ape p ſuo ſcritto de man in libretto.val.   k.1°.   §   f   g   p̃

La medema.ala m̃.e anche per la precedente i quaderno coſi.
Ð ffð.dela m̃.die hauer.a di tal p cucari de palermo cõprai va f quan danto° de meſina pla
montare de duc.tari.a tari p c°.ſenſar f quan de gaiardi monta. k.zc   §   f   g   p̃

Commo ſe debia ordinare el pagamento che haueſſe a fare per ditta e banco ð ſcritura ne
li tuoi libri principali: Cap° 19.

Coſi p tal cõpre.qſta ti baſta a guidarte.o ſia a tutti cõtanti.o a pre cõtanti.E p
retpo. o cõtati e ditta o tutti in banco.o cõtanti e banco.o cõtari.E robbe.o rob
ba.e ditta.o tutta ditta o robbe.e tpo.o robba e banco.o banco e tpo.o bãco e dit
ta.o banco.cõtanti. ditta.e robbe. zc.poche i tutti qſti modi.ſe coſtuma cõprare.
le qli tu per te.al ſeſo dela precedēte metterale imemoriale.E drigarale i giornale.cquaderno.
                                        p̃ iiij

Mà q̃do hauʼáfar pagamẽto a pte bãco e ditta. Fa cĩ p°.cõſegni la ditta.e poi p re°.ſcriui I banco.p piu figurta.vnde ancoza q̃ſta cautella ſuſa p molti e bene.q̃do ben pagaſſero á cõtanti.de far per reſto in bancho. E p cõpito pagamẽto ꝝc. E pagandolo pte.banco pte. roba .parte ditta.e parte cõtanti.de tutte q̃ſte faralo debitoze. E q̃lle tal coſe farale creditrici ognuna al ſuo luogo ꝝc. E ſe per altri modi te acadeſſe cõpzare.per ſimili te gouerna. ꝝc
    E hauẽdo intẽſo elucrſo òl cõprare p̃tanti verſi pzederai elvẽdere tuo adaltri. facẽdoſi debitozi.e creditrici leue.robbe. E debitrici lacaſſa.ſe ti da contanti.e òbitrici le ditte.ſe te le cõſegna in pagamẽto. E creditoze.el banco.ſe tel da. E coſi di tutto p ozdine cõe diſopza e ditto òl cõpzare. E lui de tutto q̃llo ti da.in pagamẽto faralo creditoze ꝝc.eq̃ſto ti baſti a q̃ ſta materia a tua inſtructiõe ꝝc. Dele pzite famoſe e pticulari nel maneggio traficãte cõe ſóno baratti cõpagnie ꝝc.cõe le ſe habbino a ſettare e ozdinare neli libzi mercãteſchi. e p°.ò li baratti ſeplici cõpoſti e coltpo cõ apti erẽpli ò tutti i memoziale.çoznale e q̃der°.   Ca.20.

E q̃ta.douer var modo.cõe ſe habino aſettar alcñe pzite famoſe pticulari. dĩ ne li maneggij traficãti ſi ſogliano elpiu dele volte.ſolẽiçare. E metterle dapſe.acio di q̃lle diſtintte valaltre.ſene poſſa cognoſcere.el p e vãno che di q̃lle ſeq̃ſſe.cõe ſóno li baratti. e lecõpag°.viaggi recomãdati.viaggi ſi ſua mano.cõmiſſiõe hauui te p altri.banchi de ſcritta.o vero ditta.E àbi reali.vinicõto de botega ꝝc. delcq̃li q̃ ſequère ſuccitamẽte a tua baſtança.te varo notitia.cõe le debi guidare.e reggere nell tuoi libzi ozdi natamẽte.acio nõ te abagli in tue facẽde. E p°.moſtzaremo cõe ſe debia aſettare 1°. baratto. Sóno libaratti cõmunamẽte de.3.ſozte cõe diſopza in leratiõ ſo detto. Diſtictio.9°.T.3°. carti.161.ſin in.167.apieno ſiche li recozri a itenderli.   Dico adõca che in tutti iuerſi che te ucadeſſe ſcriuere i lib? el baratto.ſẽpze puramẽte.p°.in lo memoziale debi narrarlo ad lfam. dèr°.oela pzita cõ tutti ſuo modi e conditiõi del ſira ſtato fatto.e cõcluſo.o comẽçant. o fra voi ſoli. E q̃do ſarai coſi narrato. E tu poi alafine riduralo i ſu licõtanti.'E ſo che q̃lle tal robbe ueder ai ualere.a cõtanti p tãto tirarai foza lapzi°.alche moneta ſi voglia i memoziale. che non fa caſo.poche poi el q̃dernieri la redura tutta a 1°.ſozta alautẽtico.cioe q̃do ſamet tara al gioznale. E al q̃derno grãde ꝝc.E q̃ſto ſi fa pche cauãdo tu fozi le valute dele robbe a q̃l che ti ſtanno abazatto.nõ potreſti nell moi cõt.e ſcripture.cognoſcere ſeça grãdiſſima difficulta.tuo vtile.o vero pditta ſequita.Eqli ſẽpze cõuiẽſi redure a cõtanti. p volerle ben cognoſcere.ꝝc.   E ſe di tali mercãtie hauute p baratti:voleſſi dapte pticularmẽte tenerne cõto.p poder veder il ſuo retratto.ſepaſamẽte va lalt°.robbe che vital ſozta haueſſe.p°.in caſa.o che vapoi cõpzaſſe.p cognoſcere qual ſia ſtata megliore icepra.lo poi fare. E àcoza acu mulare tutte mercãtie inſiemi.cõe ſe haueſſe.p°.çençeri va te. E hoza q̃ſti receueſſi vel barat to li quali voler metter con lialtri.nel çoznal virai coſi.cioe.

Per çençeri bellidi i mõte.o vero in colli: A q̃cari de latal ſozta ꝝc.p colli tanti.peſano. § tã te haui val tal abaratto de q̃cari fatto i q̃ſta fozma.cioe che mi li miſi el c°.de q̃cari duc. 24.ꝝc.cõ q̃ſto che mi deſſe e l ¾.de contanti ꝝc.E metteſe el c° di çençeri duc.tanti. p liquali çençeri.li cõ q̃cari.pani.n° tanti.peſan § tante che acontanti el c° val duc.20. E p li ditti çençari nebbe § tante ꝝc.pani n°.tanti ꝝc. vagliano ciaſcuno.   §   ℔   q̃   p̃

E pche ale volte nõ ſapzai.a põto lo n° deli pani.che p ditti çençeri intraſſe nõ fa caſo. po cõ poi nela pzita ſeq̃nte.ſi ſupleſſi q̃l che il mancaſſe.o q̃l che li foſſe piu i q̃lla dela caſſa.mãca ra nõ vimeno.alincõtro de q̃cari ſẽpze.harai el douere aponto.pche tutte dua.vãno a q̃cari i modo che laptita de q̃cari non pde el n? de pani.ne dil peſo.pche nõ e ſẽpze poſſibi le dogni fraſchetta.va pſe tener cõto.ꝝc.Oza di q̃lla pte de cõtanti che vi ſóno cozſi.fara ne debitrici lacaſſa. E pure al ſimile.creditozi ditti çucari.dicendo coſi.cioe.

Per caſſa: A li ditti ꝝc.   per contanti hebinel ditto baratto. val ditto ꝝc.per pani n°. tan ti ꝝc.peſano § tante val.   §   ℔   q̃   p̃

E ſimili pzite ſubito q̃lli mettano imediate uel gioznale a pſſo q̃lla del baratto. nel q̃l hauẽ ſti li conti ꝝc.ſi che a q̃ſto modo vittareſti.non volendone tener ſeparato conto. Oa ſe ſe parato louoi tener nel gioznale virai coſi.cioe.

Per çençeri bellidi. per conto di bazatto ſebbero val tale ꝝc: A q̃cari ꝝc. narrando tutto. poi a ponto commo diſopza. E in lo quaderno.poi barano lozo partita. viſtincta ꝝc. queſto uo gĩo che ti baſti.per tutti li altri baratti che ſo per te ſença piu mi ſtenda .ti ſapa rai guidare ꝝc.

    De laltra partita famoſa vitra Compagnie:comme ſe debino ozdinare.e vittare in tutti ſi modi occurrenti iu ciaſcuno libzo.   Cáp°. 21.

Altra partita famosa e la cōp'.cħ cō alcūo facesse p ragiōe di ǧlūdxe cola si fa
cesse o di panni o de sete o de speriarie o de gottōi e de tētoria o de cābi. zc. Que
ste talisimili sepxe uogliāo sua ptita separata i tutti li.zilibxi detti Ad p:cioe me/
moxiale posto che tu barai el di di sopxa narrarala septicimēte tutta con modi e
cōditiōi cħ lauete fatta alegan:scripto ouer altro istro cħ fra uoi fosse e noiando el tpo cħto
la sintēde:e di che faculta si fa cli fattori e garzonichxe sauesse a tenere zc.e quello che mette
ciascū perse o de robba o de ō. zc.o debitoxi o creditoxi e di tutto a vno a vno farane credi
toxi li cōp'.ognū di ǧi tanto che mette da pse e debitrici la cassa ō la dēa cōp'.se da perse la
titi cōmeg:se reggi el trafico tēndōla separata vala cassa tua pxicular ǧ:tu fosse ǧl cħ talcō'.
guidasse p la ǧl te cōuē fare lib'.vaple cō ǧllordie mō evia cħ vi sop e ōco:ō tutto el tuo ma
neggio p mē bxiga:nō vimēo potresti tutta tenerla nelli medēi toilib'. verigado noue pxite
cōmo al pxite vicemo cħ si chiamāo famose p eēr separte va tutte talt'.ō le ǧli ǧ te vo el mō
succito cōmo labi additare i tuo mēoxiale e vi poi i giornale e ǧderno zc.Ma tenēdo vi lei
lib'.sepati nō ti vo alt:vocumito senō cħ liguidi si cōmo ō tuito el tuo trafico e ōco. Dirolla
cosi ime'.   In ǧsto vi biamo sēo cōp'.cō li tali e tali alarte ō la lana zc.cō pacti e cōdutio
ni zc.cōmo ape p scripto o istro zc.p āni tāti zc.onde el tal vcxe cōtāti tāti zc.Lalt: balle
tāte lana frāc'.pesa netta ₰.tāte zc.messacōto vuc.tāti el m:zc.clalt: asegtāti veri vebito
ri.cioe el tal ve vuc.tāti.el tal ve ranti zc.e cosi io sboxfai ō pxēte vuc.rāti zc.e so i sūma;tut
to el cox.vuc.tāti zc.Poi in tuo giornale viraxi i ǧsto mado asentado rutte cose a suo luogo
imagina v'.cassa cħ compagnia cvn cauedal vi cō''.e cosi a tutte le pxite cħ tu metteraxi vixai
sēpxe p cōto ō :op'.acio labi acognoscere vαlt'.coi pxite pxiculari zc.e p'.omo festi da la caf
fa comēçaraj e poi succesfinamente asettaraj lalxre.   Per cassa ve compagnia.al tale ve ra/
gion ve compagnia aclo se hauesse altri conti con teco non simpacino zc.per contanti mi
śe I ǧsto vi p la sua rata.z:li nxi pacti cōmo apare p scripto ouer istro zc.val ₰. ſ. g° ſ̄.
Poi sumilmēte diraj de le robbe che bano messe cosi. Per lana franc'.de la cōp'.al tale p
balle tante pesano nette itutto ₰.tante fo cōta dacoxdo con tutti ducati ranti el m:secondo
la fox'. del cōtratto ouer scripto fra noi zc.mōta itutto vuc.zc.val ₰. ſ. g° ſ̄. e cosi an
daraj ponēdo tutte.p'li debitoxi cōsegnati virai cosi. Per lo tale de ragiō de cōp'. Al tale
ǧl secōdo nxi pacti cl cōsegno p vero debitoxe de duc.ranti val ₰. ſ. g° ſ̄. Ox maj
che alǧto sei itrodutto nō mi curo stēdxrme piu si cōmo in lo pncł:di ǧsto trattato feci che
troppo seria auolerte ogni cosa di nuouo replicare.E po del modo de metterle al ǧderuo
grande nō ne dico perche se o te sia facile cognoscēdo gia tu in lo giornale ǧl ua debitoxe e ǧl
creditoxe.siche asettarale tu i dare e bauere in quel modo che di sopxa i questo te isegnaj a
ca:15:e depēnarale i giornale cōmo diffi di sopxa al ca:12:ponēdo sēpxe demāce i margine
li nūcri del debitoxe e creditoxe:a ǧte carti libaraj posti al libro.e cosi cōmo tu li metti al li
bxo grande:cosi li asetta i alfabeto cōmo di sopxa piu fiade bauemo mostro zc.

De loxdine de le pxite de ciascuna spesa:cōmo de casa ordinarie:straoxdinarie:e di mer/
cantie:salarü de garzoni e factoxi cōmo sabino a scriuere:e dittare nelli libri.   ca:22.

Oltra tutte le cose ditte te ouiene bauere i tutti toi libxi ǧste pxite.cioe speli ō mer
ātia speli de casa oxdiarie spese straoxdiarie vna de itrata e viscita e vna de pxo e
dāno o uoi dire auanzi e disauāzi o utile e dāno o guadagno e pdita che rāto va
le le ǧli pxite sono sūmamēte necessarie i ogni corpo mercātelço p potere tenere sempxe
cognoscere suo capitale.e ala fine nel saldo cōmo getra el trafico zc.le ǧli ǧ seǧnte abastan/
ça chiariremo cōmo se debino guidare nelli libri. Unde ǧlla de spese mercātelche si tene
p rispecto che nō sēpxe ogni peluço si po mettere subito i la pxita de la robba che tu uendi o
cōpxi cōmo acade che da poi piu di p ǧlla ti cōuerra pagare fachini e pesadoxi e ligadoxi e
barca.e bastagi.e simili a chi vn soldo.achi.2.zc.de le ǧli volēdone fare pxicular pxita sereb
be lōgo e nō meritano la spesa poche de minimis nō curat pxtox zc.E ācoxa acade che tu a/
dopxaraj ǧlli medesimi bastagi.fachini.barca.e legatoxi i vn pōto p piu diuerse cose cōmo
istruene.cħ i sī pōto scarcādo o carcādo diuerse soxte mercārie li a fattiganca e tu li pagbi p
tutte a vn tratto che nō potresti a ogni mercāria carattare la sua spesa.E po nasci ǧsta pxi
ta chiamata spese de mercātia la ǧl sēpxe sta accesa i dare cōmo tutte lalxre speli fāno Sala
rü ancoxa de factoxi e garzoni de botega si mettano i ǧste e alcuni ne fa pxita aso posta p sa
pere i ditti che spēdano lāno zc.e poi i ǧsta. la saldano:che p nū mō nō possano essere cre/
ditrici:e ǧdo cosi le trouassi seria erroxe nel libxo.E pero i memoxiale el diraj cosi.

In quesło di babian pagato abastasi barcaroli ligadoxi.pesadoxi zc.cħ carcaro e scarca
ro zc.le tali e tali cose zc.duc.ranti zc.

                                           p iiii

Poi in lo giornale couerra dir coſi.   Per ſpeſe de mercàrie: A caſſa contati: per barche e
baſtagi corde e ligatori de le tal coſe in tutto duc̄.tàti ꝛc̄.val .8. ꝟ. ꝙ° ꝑ.   In lo q̃derno
dirai coſi.   Speſi ō mercària dē dare adi tàti p caſſa ꝛc̄.val. K. 8. ꟼ. g° ꝑ.   Quella ō
le ſpeſi di caſa ordinarie nō ſi po far ſença.E itendanſe ſpeſi di caſa ordinarie: cōmo forme
ti: vini: legne: ogli: ſale: carne: ſcarpe: copelli facture de veſte: gupponi: calçe: e ſartori ꝛc̄.be
ueraggi: bēueſtite: mance: ouer bonemani ꝛc̄.barbieri: fornaro: aquaruoli: lauature de pan
ni ꝛc̄.maſarie de cocina vaſi.bichieri. e uetri: tutti ſecchi.maſtelli.botti ꝛc̄.haueūga che mol
ti de ſimili maſarie vſino tener conto ſeparato per poter preſto trouar ſuo cōto e fāno prita
noua.cōmo ācoza tu poi fare nō che di q̃ſte ma ōi qualūde altra ti parra.ma io te amaeſtro
di quelle ē bel trafico nō po far ſença ꝛc̄.e tal prita di ſpeſi di caſa dittarala ſi cōmo e ditto
de quella de la mercātia.e ſecōdo che tu vai facēdo ſpeſe groſſe adi ꝑ di metti in li libri com
mo del formento e vini legne ꝛc̄.de le quali ancoza molti coſtumano fare prita da perſe per
poter poi ala fine de lanno o a tēpo ꝑ tpo facilmente ſapere quāto de tali cōſumano ꝛc̄. ma
per le ſpeſi piccole cōmo ſono amenuto cōprar.carne e peſci: barbieri e tragbetti ſi uol torre
o vno ouer doi duc̄.a vn tratto e tenerli da parte in vno ſachetto e di quelli andar ſpēdēdo
a menuto.Perche nō ſeria poſſibil a vna a vna di tali tener conto.E coſi dicano per li con
tanti in giornale.   Per ſpeſi di caſa. A caſſa q̃lli traffi per ſpendere amenuto in vno ſachet
to duc̄.tanti ꝛc̄.val.8. ꟼ. g° ꝑ.   E poi ſe ti pare ancoza con q̃ſte ſpeſi de caſa meter
ui le ſpeſi ſtraordinarie che non fa caſo.cōmo quādo ſpendeſſe per andare a ſolaçço: e ꝑ tra
cere alarco o baleſtro e altri giochi o perdite che ti caſcaſſero e pdeſſe robbe o denari o ch te
foſſero tolte o perdeſſe in mare o per fuochi ꝛc̄.che tutti ſimili ſintendano ſpeſe ſtraordina
rie.   Le quali ancoza ſe le voli tenere da parte ſimilmente lo poi fare e molti luſano per ſa
per netto a la fin delanno quanto bano ſpeſo de ſtraordinario per le quali anco ſ intende do
ni e preſenti che tu faceſſe ad alcuno per alcuna cagione ꝛc̄.ō le quali ſpeſe non mi curo piu
oltra ſtenderme peroche ſo certo che tu per te meglio ozmai bauendo amente le coſe dette
diuiance a ſettarai che prima non bareſti facto ſi che q̃ſte laſciando diremo del modo da
ſettare le partite de vna botega ſi nel tuo quaderno.e libri ordinarii: cōmo ſe tu voleſſe te
ner tu da te cōmo lareſti a tenere che ſia bella coſa a ſapere ſi che notale.

De lordine e mō a ſap tener vn cōto de botega i tua māo.o ad altri recōmādata e cōmo
ſe debino nelli libri autentichi del patrone e anche in quelli de botega ſeparatamente ſcriuere
e dittare.   cap.23.

Ico adonca quādo baueſſe vna botega la q̃l teneſſe fornita ala giornata for de
caſa tua e for del tuo corpo di caſa.alora ꝑ bono ordine tirrai q̃ſto nō: cioe de
tutte le robbe che tu ui metterai adi ꝑ di farala debitrici ali toi libri e creditrici
q̃lle tal robbe d vi metti.a vna ꝑ vna e fa tua imagiatiōe ch q̃ſta botē.ſia vna ꝑ
ſona.tua debitrici di q̃l tāto che li dai e ꝑ lei ſpēdi i tutti li modi.E coſi ꝑ lauerſo de tutto q̃l
lo ch ne caui e receui farala creditrici cōmo ſe foſſe vn ōbitoze ch ti pagaſſe apte apte.E poi
ogni uolta che tu voli con lei cōtare tu pozrai vedere cōmo ella te butta.o bene o male ꝛc̄.E
coſi poi ſaprai q̃llo arai a fare e ch mō larai a gouernare ꝛc̄.E molti ſono ch ali ſoi libri fā
no debitoze el principale che li atēde a ditta botega beche q̃ſto nō ſi poſſa debitamente ſeça
volūta di q̃l tale.poch mai ſi deue mettere ne ācoza de ragiō ſi puo pozre vn debitore alib°
ſeça ſua ſaputa ne ācb creditoze cō cōditiōi alcūe ſeça ſua uolūta le q̃l coſe facedole tu ſere
ſti māco che da bene.E li toi libri ſerēno reputati falſi.e coſi ō le maſarie ch i q̃lla meteſſe e
ordegni neceſſarii al a ditta botega ſecōdo ſua occurēça: cōmo ſe foſſe ſpeciaria ti conuerra
formirla ō vaſi.caldieri.ramini.da lauorare ꝛc̄.di q̃li tutti farala debitrici o colui che li attē
de cōmo ditto.e ꝑ bello iuētario li le aſegna ſcripto ō ſua māo o d altri ō ſua uolūta ꝛc̄. acio
de tutto ſia bē chiaro.e q̃ſto voglio ſia baſtāte q̃do la botega baueſſe conſegnata a vn altro
ch ꝑ te la faceſſe o foſſe tuo cōmeſſo ꝛc̄.Ma ſe la dca botega vozrai tener a tuoi mài q̃ſto oz
die fuarai e ſtara bene. e metiamo ch cōpri e traficbi tutto ꝑ la ditta botega e nō baui altr°
maneggio alora formarai li libri commo e ditto.E di cio che vendi e compri farai credito
ri chi te da le robbe per tanto tempo ſe compri a tempo e creditrici la caſſa ſe compri a con
tanti e debitrici la botega.E quando tu vendeſſe a menuto.cioe che non ariuaſſe a.4.0.6.du
cati ꝛc̄.alora tutti ditti denari repozrai in vna caſſetta.ouer ſalua denaro dōde i capo ō.8.o
10.giozni li ne canarai.e alora farāe debitrici la caſſa e credetrici la bo°.di q̃l tāto: e i la prita
dirai ꝑ piu robbe vēdute de le q̃li gia bauerai tenuto el cōto e molte altr° coſe in le q̃li nō mt.

uoglio troppo distendere:p che lo cómo disopra diffusaméteb abiáo dcó ormai sapzai perte
itederle cóciosia che cóti non sóno altro che vn debito ordine o: la fantasia che si fa el mercatante per el qual uniforme seruato puene ala notitia de tutte sue faccde e cognosci facilméte p qllo se le sue cose uáno bene o male.p che el prouerbio dici chi fa mercátia e nò la cognosca li soi denari douétan mosca &c.e secódo le occurrence li fa remedio, E pero piu e má
co li sipo sempre agiongere in numero e i multitudine de pate.E po de qíto tacótcta.

Cómo se babino aletrare nel giornale e quaderno le parate de li báchi de scritta:eqli se i
rédino e doue ne sia:o de cábi:tu cólozo siandomercatáte:e tu có áltri qdo fosse báchieri:
e de le quie táge che p li cábi se fáno. e p che sene facia doi de medesimo tenore   ca ,24

Ora per li banchi de scripta ō quali se ne troua oggi di inuinetia i bruggia sauer-
sa e barçelóa e certi altrituoghi famosi e traficáti ti cóué sap có lozo libzi scótra-
re có grádissima diligétia. E peroe da notar che có lobancho te poi cómunamé
te impaciare da te ponédoui denari per piu tua sigurecça:o uero p modo de di-
poiito a la giornata poter con quelli far tuoi pagamenti chiari apiero gioáni e martino per
che la oitta del bancho e comme publico iltruméto de notaro p che son per li dominij aff
guratt onde ponédoui tu oa te.ō.farai debitore ditto bancho nominaudo patroni o uero
cópagni del bácho e creditrici la tua cassa cosi dicédo i giornae   Per bancho de li pamani: A cassa per cótanti li misi có tali.io o altri che per me fosse in quelto di de mio conto fra
oro e moneta &c.i tutto ducati &c. Ual. §.F.g.p. E farate fare oal banchieri doi uersi suno
soglio p piu cautela. E cosi giongédogline tu ala giornata farai el simile: cauandone tu lui
te fara scriuere a te el receuere:e cosi le cose si uengano sempze a mátener chiare: Uero e che
aleuolte tal scritte nó si costumano p che cómo e ditto li libri del bancho sempze sóno publi
che autentiche:ma pur e buonola cautela p che cómo disopza so detto al mercante le cose
mai forō.troppo chiare. Ma se tu uolesse tal pŭta tenerla con li patroni:o uero cópagni del
bancho ancoza lo poi fare de tanto uale po che noiando tu el bácho a modo disopza sinté
de li patrói e cóp°.de quello: per li patróni direîti cosi.   Per miser Birolimo lipamani dal
bancho e cópagni qdo fossero piu. A cassa ut supra sequita tutto. E sempze farai neli tuoi libzi mentione de le chiarece:patti:e códitioni che fra uoi nascessero cómo de scripti de má: e
del luogo doue ti reponi i fisça:scatola:tascha:o cassa acio possi facilméte retrouare:po che
có bona diligéça simili scripture si debono seruare. ad ppetuam rei memoriá;p li picoli oc
cozzano &c. E p che aleuolte có lo báchieri pozresti bauerui piu faccde e mancggi i mercá
tia p te o per altri cómo cómesso &c.po sempze cú lui ti cóué tener cóti diuersi p non intriga
re lance có rondtoni che nascería grá confussione:e dire i le tue pute p cóto de la tal cosa:o
p cóto del tal o p ragió de mercantia o p ragion de contanti depositati i tuo nome o daltri
cómo e ōtto:le quali cose so p tuo igegno ormai reggerai &c. E similíte te reggerai saltri te
aconciasse ō.a te pcbe cóto si uolesse:farato debitoze altrui libro p ql tal cóto:cioe ō pagamé
to noiando p pte o p restoze.e ql tale farai creditoze p lo medesimo cóto e stara bene.E ą
do tu de dcó bancho cauasse.ō.i cótánti o p paga méti che adaltri facesse p pte o resto o uero
p remettere a daltri i altri paesi &c.aloza farai el cótrario de ql che finoza e dcó:cioe se caui
cótanti farai debitrici la tua cassa:e creditoze el bancho o uer patrói di quel tanto che ne ca
uasti.E se tu li scriuesse adaltri farai debitoze ql tale e creditoze detto bancho o patrói i ql
tanto noiando el pdxe dicédo i giornale p li cótanti cosi.   Per cassa al bancho o uer miser girolimo li pamani p contanti i tal di.o i qíto di ne trassi a mio bilogno &c.i tutto.duc.
táti &c.ual. §.F.g.p. E le adaltri li scriuesse uputa amartio di ĩfti cosi.   Per matt° del ta
le. Al ditto ut supra per duc.táti &c.li scrissi p pte o p resto o abō cóto o.p ipxesto &c. i qíto
di.ual. §.F.g.p.E cosi leuádo oitte pritte ōl giornale sépre a suo luogo i qderno aserrarai e:e
i alfabeto cómodi disopza dati e depénandole cómo to mostro in memoriale e giornale.p.e
mancbo per te stesso giógnédoli parolle.po che non e possibile q de tutto a pieno narrare
si che conuié dal tuo cáto sia uigilate &c. El medesimo mō te couerra obseruare p remette
re li cábi altroue.cómε lon°:brugia:ro°:lió &c.per ritrar daltro &c.nominando li°c rermi-
ni &c.o ala uista o aladata o al suo piacere cómo se costuma facédo métione de p².2°.c.3°. &c.
acio non nasca errore fra te el tuo respondente e de le monete che tu trai e rimetti e le lor
ualute e .puisiói e spesi oám e iteressi che ci li pzotesti poderebono nascere &c.i che di tutto
si uol far métione el p che e cóme. E cóme o messo che tu babi afare con bácho:cosi uersa uice
prédi se fosse tu el bancbiert mutatis mutandis che quando pagbi fa debitore quel tale e la
tua cassa creditrici e sel tuo creditore sença cauare.ō.adaltri li scriuesse dirai nel tuo giozni

le per quel tale tuo creditoxe a quel tale acbi lui li acõcia.e cofi vieni a far cõmutatione da vno
creditoxe a unaltro e tu rimani pure debitoxe e vieni in qfto atto effere perfona meggana e cõ
muna.cõmo teftimonio e factoxe de le parti a tuo inchioftro carta fitto fatiga e tempo fi che
di qua fi caua la bonefta.puiffiõe nel cambio effere fempxe licita qdo mai nõ ui cozriffe pico
lo de uiaggio altre remeffe in mano ve terge pfone ꝛc.cõmo nelli cambi reali in qfto a fuo
luogbo eftato apieno detto ꝛc.Oba fiando bãcbieri ricozdate nell ifaldi cõ toi creditozi far
te tozmare fogli pulige o altri fcripti che di tua mano baueffe de leqli quando ne fai fempxe fan
ne nel tuo libzo mentiõe acio te recozdi a fartele tozmare e ftragarli:acio nõ ueniffe a tẽpo cõ
qlli altri a domandarte e fatte fare fempxe bone quietange cõmo coftumano fare chi attẽde al
cãbio·.po che fare lufanga e che fe tu vieni.verbi gfa da gineuera con vna di cãbio q in vfa.a miff
giouãnifrefco baldi da fio².e·cõpa².cõ alauifta o data:o a tuo piacere te doueffe pagare metia
mo duc. 100.p altre tanti che dila baueffe nele man de chi li fcriue cõ fegnati:aloza el ditto
miff.giouãni e cõp².acceptãdo la lfa:e lbozfciãdote ditti.õ.te fara fcriuere õ tua mano doi de
tange de vn medefimo tenoxe:e fe tu nõ fapeffe fcriuere le far vn terço ptẽ o fxo notaro:
nõ fa cõ tentara duna p che luna cõuiẽ che rimandi a ql banchieri a gineuera:che li fcriue
che a te p fuo cõto pagbi li ditti ouc.100.i farli fede cõmo cozxefcmẽte a fatto ql tanto che
li fcriffe i cui fede in una fuali mãda laquietaça vi tua mano:e laltra tene i filça apzeffo vi fe:
acio qdo cõtaffe cõ lui non poteffe negarlilo:e di la ancoza tu tozmãdo nõ poteffe.lamẽtare
vi lui ne ve miff giouãni po che fe tu lo feffe el te moftraria vetta quietança vi tua mano e re
marefti confufo:fi che tutte qfte cofe fonno cautele che fi tonuengano ve neceffita fare p la
poca fede fi troua oggi vi vel quale atto ne nafcano voi ptite i lo qderno loro.vna in ql vi
meff giouãni facẽdo õbitoxe ql che li fcriue p vigoxe ve la vicãbio:e laltra i qllo vel refpõde
te a gineuera facẽdo creditoxe miff giouãni vi quelli ouc.100.per virtu ve vitta tua quietaça
receuuta.e quefto e el vebito modo e ozdine ve cambiatozi p tutto el mõdo: acio le loz cofe
vadino cõ cbiarecçe:fi che dal tuo lato alquãto affatigandote pozrai ogni cofa con fumma
diligença afettare.ꝛc.

    De unaltra partita che ale uolte fe coftuma nel qderno tenere entrata e·ufcita e ale
uolte fenefa libro partieulare:e per che.   ca.25.

    Onno alcuni che ne loz libzi ufano tenere vna ptita vetta entrata e vfcita i la ql
põgano cofe ftraozdinarie o altre cõmo ala. fantafia pare. Altri ne tirra una õ
fpefe ftraozdinarie e i fimili mettano cõmo i qlla vintrata iffita pfẽti che li foffer
fatti.⁊.gfa.e cofi fcõo che riceuano e vãno e tẽgano cõto i dare e bauere e poi a
la fine cõ laltre le faldãno i.p e dãno e caudale cõmo itenderai nel bilancio ꝛc.Oba i uero
qlla vetta vi fopza fpefe di cafa p tntte e baftãte fe nõ chi uoleffe per fua curiofita tener con
to da p fe fin a vn põtale de ftrẽga che lo pozria fare ma acb fine:epo fi vba a le cofe cõ bze
uita afettarfe.Altri luogbi coftuma ve litrata eufcita tener vn libzo a fua pofta:e poi quello
faldano a tẽpo vel bilãcio nel vltimo autẽtico iffiemi cõ le altre facẽde:laql cofa non e vabiaf
mare auẽga fia de piu fatiga.

    Cõmo fe babino afettare neli libzi le ptite ne li uiaggi i fua mano:e quelle ve li viaggi re
comandati:e cõmo di neceffita ve tali nafcono doi quaderni   ca.26.

    I uiaggi fi coftumano fare i voi modi:cioe i fua mano e recomandato.'vnde na
fcano diuerfi modi i tener loz cõti po che fempxe fi profupõgano libzi doppi:o fia
i tua mano o fia recõmandato.·perche luqderno refta i cafa e laltro ti cõuẽ fare
i uiaggio.vnde fel ditto viagio fia i tua mano p bõ ozdine de ciocbe tu pozti forma
tuo iuẽtario qdernetto:giozmaletto ꝛc.tutto cõmo di fopza fe vetto:e uẽdẽdo cõpzãdo ba
ratãdo ꝛc.ve tutto fa debitori e creditozi pfone:robbe: caffa:caudal:ve uiaggio:e p e van
no ve uiaggio ꝛc.e qfto e lo piu fcbietto e vica cõ fi uogbia altri. Auẽga cõ pozrefti tener cõ
to cõ la cafa dalaql tu togli la faculta che al ditto uiaggio pozti facẽdola nel libxetto vel tuo
uiaggio creditrici:e le robbe vebitrici a una p v²:e cofi fozmarefti tua caffa:ruo caudale ꝛc.
ozdenatamẽte cõmo nel tuo famofo.E tozmãdo a falua micõ rẽdarefti alacafa altre robbe ali
contro.o uero.õ.e cõ lei faldarefti cõto e lutile o vãno fegto afettarefti a fuo luogbo nel qua
derno grãde.ficbe aqfto modo ancoza le tue facẽde uercbono cbiare.Oba fel viaggio recõ
mãdaffe adaltri:aloza farefti de tutto nel tuo libro debitore ql tale acbi larecomãdi vicẽdo
per uiaggio recomãdato al tale ꝛc.e cõ lui terrefti conto cõme fe foffe vn tuo auẽtore ve tut
te robbe:e õ.a ptita per partita ꝛc.E lui dal cãto fuo fozmara fuo qdernetto:e iqllo te con
uerra fare creditore de tutto.E retornãdo faldara conteco.E fel tuo cõmeffo foffe i le bãde

De 1ª.prita famoſa vitta ,p e vāno o vero auançi e defauançi.cōe laſabia a tenere vel ǭder-
no.e pcbe clla nō ſi metta nel coznale comme le altre ptite   Cap°. 17

Eǭta voppo ognialtr° ptiª.1ª.cbiamata de ,p e vāno ovoi vire vrile e vāno ſeǭto
o vero auançi e defauāçi fo alcūo paeſe ilaǭle tutte lalt°.vel tuo ǭder: ſēp ſe ba
no a ſaldare cōe nel bilācio ſe dīra.E ǭſta nō biſogna ſimetta i giomale. ma-ba
ſta ſolo nel ǭder° pcb lanaſci i ǭllo vle coſe auāçate o vero mācate i dare e bēre
p laǭle vtrai ,p e vanno vie vare. E ,p e vāno vie bēre.cioe ǭdo valcūa robba bauelle pdu
to.lacui ptiª.piu nel tuo ǭderno reſtaſſe i vare cb i bēre.aloza aiutarai el ſuo bēre p pegiar
la al vare acio ſe ſaldi.ve ǭl tanto cbe li mancaſſe.vicēdo. e vie bēre p ,p e vāno ǭl ǭ metto
p ſaldo ve ǭſta.p vanno ſeǭto zc.e ſegnarai lecarti ōl ,p e danno nel traz fuoza laptiª.E al
,p e vāno andarai i vare.vicēdo ,p e vāno vie vare a vi zc.p latal robba.p vanno ſeǭto tan
to zc.poſto i ǭlla aldie bēre p ſuo ſaldo ape acarti zc.E ſe la foſſe piu i bēre vitta robba cb
i dare.aloza fareſti plo aduerſo..E coſi andarai facēdo a 1ª.p 1°.ve tutte robbe finite. o ma
le o bñ cb ſiēno andate acio ſēpze.eltuo ǭderno ſe ritroui paro ve ptiª.cioe cb tante ſene tro
ui i vare ǭte i bēre.pcb coſi ſedeue ritrouare a ſtar bñ çoe ſe vtra nel bilancio. E coſi ſuccin
ta mēre vedarai ſe guadagni o ꝓo pdi e ǭto.E ǭſta ptita.poi ancoza lei ſi cōuerra ſaldare
i çoznale bēcb ſi potrebbe acbi voleſſe e verria a reſpōdere ancoz bñ.ma nō fa biſog°.pcb
ſe bēria ǭlla fatica.piu ſēça frutto.ſicbe biſogna aiutar la minor ǭª.cioe ſele,piu in dare cb i
bēre vitta ptiª.vi ǭl tanto aiuta el ſuo bēre zc.E p erª.cbiaro tenemettaro ǭ 1ª. e mettiamo
cbe Cbartino babia fatto cō teco cōto lōgo ve piu ptiª.i modo.cbe laſua poſta ſia.varepoz-
tare.eſia nel tuo ǭder°.a carti.30.e lultiª.ptirª.ve tutto el ǭder°.ſia a carti.60.i ǫima.c ala me
deſima façata ſia luogo vapoterui ancoza locare ǭlla ve CPart°.E ſiate ōbito cl vitto 8. 80
f 15.g.15 p̄.24.veliǭli in tutto te nabia vato.8 72.ſ 9.g.3.p̄.17.vico cbe batta cl ſuo bēre ōl
ſuo vare.cioe. 72.9.3.17.reſta. 8 8 f 6 g.5 ꝑ 7.E ve tanto lo veui poztar vebitoze auanti. E
ve ǭllo medeſimo veui aiutrare laprita in bēre.e vitrai coſi.avi.zc.p lui medeo ǭl poſto auan
ti in ǭſto aloia vare p reſto ǭl pōgo ǭ p ſaldo. 8 8 f 6 g 5 ꝑ 7. val a carti.60.8 f g.p̄. ōpēne
rai laptiª. in vare e in bēre cō 1ª.linea viametraliter.E fatto ǭſto andarai a carti.60.in vaſ
Epozrai vitto reſto pōnēdo ſēpze viſop°.p².ſenō cl foſſe el CD: cōe vinançe fo vitto.E-vi-
rai coſi.CDartino vie vare a vi zc.p lui medemo p reſto tratto va vzieto in ǭſto poſto aldie
bēre p ſaldo ō ǭlla. val acarti.30.8 8 f 6 g 5 ꝑ 7.E ǭſto medeſi° modo obſuarai in tutte ptie
cbe baueſſe a repoztare auanti incatenandole al modo vitto e ſēça interuallo alcūo.po cb ſe
pze le ptie°.ſi vogliano ponere cōe naſcano ō luogo.ſito.vi.e mileſi° acio niſū te poſſi calu-
niare.zc.   Del modo a ſapere mutare el mileſimo nel quaderno fra le partite cbe ala çoz
nata acaſcano.quando ogni anno nōn ſi ſaldaſi li libzi.   Capitolo. 29.

Orria cſb alcuolte cbe nele tue ptite in quaderno. tu baueſſi a mutar mileſi° E
nō,baueſſe ſaldato.aloza vitto mileſi°.veui ponere in margine ariperto vitra pri
ta cb coſi e nata.cōe fo vetto ſopza in.cap.15°.E tutte lalte cbe la ſeǭteranno ſe
intēderanno al vitto mile° CBa ſēpze e buono veſaldare ognanno.maxime cbi
e in cōpª.pcbe el puerbio vici ragion ſpeſſa amiſta lōga.E coſi farai a tutte ſimili.

Comme ſe vebia leuare vn conto al vebitoze cbe lo vomandaſſe.e ancoza al ſuo patrōe
ſiando fatoze e commeſſo ve tutta la aminiſtratione de le robbe   Capitolo. 30.

Iſogna oltra li vati vocumēti.ſape leuare vncōto al tuo debitoze cb te lo domā
daſſe. El ǭle nō ſi po de ragion negare. pſtim ǭdo cō teco baueſſe tenuto conto
lōgo. de piu anni e meſi zc.aloza farate da przn° cb inſiemi baueſte afare.o da al
tro termine cb lui el voleſſe ǭvo fra voi foſſero ſtari altri ſaldi va ǭl tpō cb lovo
le per vna volta volentieri li le leua. E de tutto farai vna partita in vn foglio cbe ui capa.
E ǭdo in.1ª. facia non capiſſe ſaldarai otro quello cbe li bauerai pozto. e pozterai el vitto
valaltro lato del foglio in dare.overo bauere commo nel capitolo.28°. fo detto.E va con-
tinuando.E a lultimo.redullo in reſto netto ovna ſola partita in dare. o bzaucr ſeconda
cbe lanaſcera. E queſti tali conti ſi vogliano leuare con grandiſſima vuligentia.

E qfto modo obfuarai neli fatti tuoi ,ppri.e tuoi auctori. CBa fe tu amiftraffe p altrı. p ufa
de acomáde.o de cómifiói.aloza fimilméte cofi lo leuar.ai al patróe cóe ò póto lbarai poſto
al libzo.facèdote creditoze de tpo i tpo dele tuoi ,puifiói fo vii parti.E poi i fine p refto net
to.del rirratto.farate fuo debitoze.o vro creditoze qdo del tao libaueffe meffo.e lui poi lo re
uedara.pótádolo. có lifuoi. E trouádolo ſtar bene.te vozra meglio.E piu te fidara.p debi
fogna che de tutto qllo te a dato o mandato che del reccuere a lfe di tua mano li ne afegni
aminiſtrationi ordinatamête.E po nota bene. E p lauerfo farai tu leuarlo a tuoi fattori. o
vero cómeffi fimiliter. CBa p².che foza fe vieno li conti fi uogliano ben pontare có tutte lo
ro prite i qderno i gioz|nale e memoziale.E con tutti luoghi che laueffe fcritte acio nó nafcе
fe erroze fra le pti.   Del modo e ordine a fape retrattare.o vero iſtoznare i².o piu prite
che p erroze haueffe poſte i alt° luogo cb doueffero ádare cóe auene p fméoragie. Cap° xı.

Ancoza neceffario al bon quadernieri fapere retrattare. o voi dire ſtoz|na
re ala fiorentina vna partita che per erroze haueffe poſta in altro luogo che el
la doueffe andare. comme fe laueffe meffa in dare. E douiala ponere in bauere
Et econtra.E quando douia poz|la acónto de CBartino E lui la miffe a conto
de quani.et ecótra.Pero che ale volte non fi po tanto effere arento che non fi falli comme al
prouerbio fona. Cioe chi non fa non falla. E chi non falla non impara. E pero inretrat)
tarla.tirrai qſto modo.Cioe qdo haueffe meffa laprita.poniamo.i dare e douia andare in
bauere p retrala poz|raine i².alt°.alicontro deffa i bauere de ql tanto de ponto. E dirai.in q
ſto modo a di.7c.p altretanto poſto dincontro al die dare.E douia metterla di i bauere|val
a carti 7c.E tra foza qlle mdefime.§.§.g.p.che poneſti p erro.E denanze a ditta prita farai
i².croci.o altro fegno. acio leuando tu el cóto lauęgbi alaffare.E fubito poſta qſta p retrat
to.cb e qſto fenulla haueffe fcrito del deuere. fi tu poi la reponi i ditto bauere cóe douia an
dare eſtara bñ.   Comme fi debbia fare elbilancio del libzo e del modo a reportare vn
libzo in laltzo.cioe el qderno vecchio nel quaderno nuouo e del modo a pontarlo con lo fuo
giozinale e memoziale e altri fcontri détro e difuoze del ditto quaderno.   Cap°.   xı.

Queſte cofe finoza bé notate bifogna bora dar modo al reporto de vn libzo in lal
tro.qdo uoleffe mutar libzo. p cagione che foffe pieno o vero p ordine annuale
de mileſimo cóe el piu fi coſtuma fare p luochi famofi che ogni anno. marime
amileſiini-nuoui li gran mercatanti fępze lo obfuano. E qſto atto infiemi con li
feqnti.E detto elbilancio del libro.Eaqll cofa voler fedre.bifogna grandiffima diligétia.e p
ordine tirrai qſto modo.cioe P°.farai de bauere vn cópagno.che mal pozreſti p e folo far
lo.E alui darai in mano el giozinale p piu tua cautella. E tu tirrai el qderno grande e dirai
alui gomêcando dala p°.prita del giozinale che chiami le carti del tuo qderno. doue qlla
fia poſta.p°.i dare e poi i bauere.E cofi lu lubbidirai.E trouerai fępze doue te manda. E ql
te dira la prita de cb o de chi la fira. E qſto fia eſſuo tratto foze. E coſi tuvedarai i ql tal luo
go doue te manda.fe bauerai ql cb.o ql chi. E ql tanto apoſto trattto foze.E trouodádola
ſtare aponto cóe i giozinale láncarala.cioe pontazala. overo farai qlche fegno alibito i fu le
§.o altroue che non te abagliaffe.E ql tal fegno o vero láncata che cofi in altri luochi fi co
ſtuma dir.dirai che faça.elcópagno nel giozinale.ala medefima pri². E guarda che mai tu fe
ça lui ne lui fença te pótaffe.overo láçaffe prita alcũa pche pozrebe nafcere grádi errozi. po
che la prita pórata che fia vol dire ſtar bñ.col debito modo. E qſto ancoza fe obfua i leuar
de conti a debicoi nançe che li te vaglbi in mano bauerlo fcótrato e pontato có li luochi dl
qderno e del giozinale o daltri luochi che aueffe notate ditte prite cóe fopza al.30.ca° fo dt
to. E fatto qſto p ordine a tutto el qderno e giozinale. E trouando tu aponto cóc lui i dare e
bauere le prite firan giuſte e ben poſte. Noza cb lui nel giozinale p bona memoria fara dol
láncate o vero póti a i².fola prita.E tù nel qderno uſei folo afarne i².p pti². fi cóe duna pri²
de giozinale in qderno fene fa doi cofi fi fa doi pontı.E po nel pontare del bilancio i giona
le acb e buono far doi póti lũo fotto lalt°.ale §.o uero doi láçate i². fotto lalt°.cb dinora dit
ta pri².ſtar bñ i dare e bère al qder° Alcũi nel giozinale p lodare pótano dauáti al.p.E p lo
bauere dzieto ale c..cóe fe fia lũo e lalt°. ſta bñ. Nó dimeno fi pozria far ácoza có i².pótatu
ra fola i giozinale.cioe folo p lo dare.pche tu poi per teſteffo pozreſti pontare lbauere a qual
partita che hai tu voleffe fempre tu le manda per che fubito tu bai qiuſi el numero
dele carti doue ſta lbauere quando bene quel del giozinale non te mandaffe fiche fcontran
dote tu con lui folo indare per te ſteffo pozreſti fequire lo bauere ma piu commodo te fia có
lo compagno a modo ditto.CBa fe formito el giozinale de pórare a te auancaffe in quaderno
prita alcũa che non ueniffe pórata in dare o in bauere denotaria nel quaderno eſkr errof.
cioe che qlla fcraue poſta fupflua in ql dare o vero bauere.elqual erroze tu fubito retratta-

rai vædo lamedefima q̃°.alincontro.cioe fe la fira ve piu in vare. E tu altre tanto porrai in
bauere. Et ecõtra. laq̃lcofa cõe fabia adittare vifopra te fo vetto al cap°. pcedête. E cofi ba
rai medicato tutto.El medefimo feria q̃do lui baueffe in giornale prita fupflua. cĥe a te nel
quaderno mãcaffe in vare o in bauere cĥe pur fallo nel quaderno venotarebbe. El quale fi
veue repare al modo contrario vel fupfluo.Cioe cĥe tu alora vitta prita fubito laponghi l
vare e in bauere in quaderno.faccendo mêtione vela varieta vel corno.pcĥe lanafcera molto piu tarda in quaderno.cĥe nõ voui. Dele quali varieta.fêpre elbõ quaderniero veue far
ne mêtione pcĥe lenafcĥino p leuar ilfufpetto vel lib°.amodo el bon notaro neli fuoi inftru
mêti.nequali non po ne grongnere ne fmínuire fença priculare mêtione ve tal augumêto. o
vero vecremento.cofi fêpre tal refpetto cõufê cĥe fia nel bon quadernieri. acio la rialita mer
cantefca.vebitamête fe venga amaxterière.Qa fe la vitta prita.folo mancaffe val vare o vâ
lbauere.alora bafta la ponghi i°.fola volta.va q̃l tal lato voue lamancaffe.con vitte mentio
ni.Cioe cõe p errore lai fatto ꝛc. E cofi barai tutte q̃ftate tue prite.lequali trouandole a fol
fcontri cõe e vifcorfo venota eltuo quaderno eêr giufto e ben tenuto.Unde nota cĥe nel dit
to quaderno firâno a leuolte molte prite non pontate con lo fcontro vel giornale p cĥenon
fi bano aritrouare ineffo. E q̃fte firãno li refti pofti al vie dare.o in bauere p faldi vele p ꞏ
tite nel portarle bauanti cõe vicêmo in lo cap°.28.alora va te fteffo vi q̃lli tali refti trouerai
i.vitto q̃derno fuoi fcontri.cioe in vare. E in bauere.recêdote p lo n°. ve le carti cĥ ila vitta
prita notate firâno. E trouãdo fcontro a fuoi luoghi gudica fimilmête elq̃derno ftar bñ ꝛc.
E q̃llo cĥe finoza fe detto del fcõtro vel quaderno con lo giornale.el fimile intêdi p°.douerfi
fare del memoriale ó vero fquartafoglio cõ logiornale a di p di. q̃do vfaffi tener memozia
le a modo cĥe in principio di q̃fto trattato de lui te dixi.e cofi cõ tutti altri libri teneffe.Qa
lultimo conuen effere elquaderno.cio penultimo el giornale.Ideo ꝛc.

Del modo e ordine afcriuere lefacende cĥe occureffero nel tempo cĥe fi fa elbilancio.cioe
cĥe fi faldano li libri.e comme neli libri uecĥi nõ fi vebia fcriuere ne innouare cofa alcuna
in vitto tempo e lacagione perchc.   Cap°.   33.

Utte q̃fte cofe ordinatámente fatte e obferuate.guarda non innouaffe piu prî°
in alcũ libro antiano al quaderno.cioe immemoziale. E giornale.perchc el faldo
tutto ve tutti li libri fêpre fi veue intendere fatto in i°.medefimo corno Qa fe fa
cende te acaveffe in q̃l mecço cĥe fai el tuo faldo o vero bilancio. porrale in libri
nuoui nequali intêdi fare reporto.cioe in lomemoziale o vero giornale.ma nõ in quaderno
p fin tanto cĥe non li hai portati li refti vel p° quaderno. E fe ancora non baueffe ordinati
libri nuoui porrai le facêde con li fuoi corni vapre in i°.f foglio p fin firan fatti vitti libri. E
alora li leporrai.fignati cĥe firan tutti ve nuouo fegho. E fe q̃lli cĥe faldi firâ fegnati.cro
ci q̃fti fegna de. A.ꝛc.   Côme fe vebiano faldare tutte leptite vel q̃dernoverbio.e i cĥi
e pcĥe:e de la ffima fũmarũ vel vare e velauere vltio fcontro vel bilãcio.   Cap°.   34.

Atto cĥ barai q̃fto cõ vilegêtta. E tu vate faldarai tutto eltuo q̃derno aptira p
prî°.i q̃fto modo.cĥ p°.comêçarai valacaffa vebitori.robbe e auentori. E quelle
porrai in libro. A. cioe in quaderno nuouo cĥe non bifogna cõe fo vetto vifo
pra lirefti ponere ingiornale. fummarai tutte loz prite in dare e bauere aiutãdo
fêpre lamenore cõe te viti. fopra vel portare auãti.cĥe q̃fto atto ve ꞏ i° quaderno in laltro.E
ve pôto fimile aq̃llo e fra loro non e altra vifferentia fenon cĥe in q̃llo virefto fi porta auan
ti nel medefimo quaderno. E in q̃fto ve ꞏ i° libro in laltro. E voue un q̃llo cĥiamani le carti v̂
q̃l libro °pprio in q̃fto fichĥama lecarti vel libro fequête in modo cĥe nel reporto ve vn libro
in laltro.folo i°.uolta p ciafcũ quaderno fe mette laprita. E q̃fta progatiua a lultima prita
fempre veli quaderni cĥe nullaltra mai po bauere cõe nel pceffo vato hai notato. E veueffe
tal riporto cofi vitare.cioe mettiamo cĥe tu habia.Qartino vebitore p refto nello tuo qua
derno.crocĩ.a carti.60.ve.8 12.ŝ 15.g 10.ꝓ 26. E habilo a portare in quaderno. A. a carti. 8:
in dare e connen nel libro croci.alutare lbauere.voue dirai cofi defotto a tutte laltre partite
E a di ꝛc.ponêdo fempre el medefimo di.cĥe fai elbilancio. p lui medemo porto in quader
no. A. aldie dare per refto qual q̃ pôgo per faldo de quefta val acarti.8.8 12.ŝ 15. g 10.ꝓ 26
E depennarai la vitta partita in dare e bauere diametraliter cõe nel reporto te infegnai po
nêdo laffima de tutta laptita fotto nel cãpo de vitta prita in dare e in bêre.cioe tãto da fuo
lato q̃to da lalt°.acio pa a lochio fubito ftar bñ e iq̃le cõe fe recerca:al bõ faldo. ponêdo nel
trar fora.el numero dele carti vel quaderno. A. voue tal refto porti. E poi in lo quaderno.
A. in dare dirai cofi prima ponendo fopra incima de la carta.el fuo milefimo.El giorno ne
lapartita per lacafone detta fopra in lo cap.15°.cioe Qartino deltale ꝛc.die dare a di ꞏ3°ꝓ

lui medemo p resto tratto del libro.croci.posto al die batere per saldo de qlla.val a car. 6o.
$ 12.§ 15.g° 1o.p 26.E cosi andarai saldãdo tutte le prite nel lib°.croci.cõ tu intẽdi portare
i qderno. A. de cassa.caucdal.robbe mobili. e stabil.debitori.creditori.officii.sensarie. pesa
don de comun zc. con liquali se vsa ale volte andare aconto lóngo zc. Ona quelle partite
che non volesse portare in ditto quaderno. A. che portieno eẽre qlle che solo a te saprẽga
no.E nõ se obligato a segnarne cõto ad alcu? cõe son spesi de mercãtia.spesi de casa intrata
isita.e tutte spese straordinarie.fitti.pesciõi.feudi. o liuelli zc.qste simili conuẽgonse saldare
in lo medesimo libro.croci.ncla prita del .p e danno o vero anãçi e desauançi o voi dire vti
le e dãno.i qsto modo che loro dare portarai i dare cõ raro si possano hauere i credito qlle
dcle spesi dicẽdo.nel saldo aiutando cõe piu volte ditto sempre lamenore quantita in dare
o i hauere p .p c dãno i qsto a carti tãte zc. E cosi tutte le hauerai saldate i qsta del .p e dan
no doue subito poi sũmando suo dare e haucre porrai cognescere tuo guadag°.e pdita p cõ
sira i tal bilancio fatto la parita.cioc qlle le cose cõ se douiã diffalcare siran diffalcate qlle che
se douiano agiongnere sirã .pporrtionatamẽte a suoi luochi agiõte.E se de qsta ptita.sira p
el dare cõ lauere tu hauera pdutto ql tanto i tuo trafico dache lo gomẽçasti.E se sia piu lo
hauere aloza dirai che ql tanto hahia i ditto tpo guadagnato zc.E veduto cõ harai p qsta
sutile.e danno tuo sedro.alora qsta saldarai i lapita del cauedale.doue nel pricipio del tuo
manegio ponesti lo iuẽtario de tutta la tua faculta.E saldarala i qsto.modo che sel dãno se
qto sira piu che dio ne guardi ciascuno che realmẽte sobuon xpiano se adopa aloza aiuta
rai lohauere amodo visto dicẽdo e a di zc.p cauedal i qstop danno sedro a carti zc.val zc.
E depẽnerai lapita diametraliter i dare e hauere.vt sua.ponẽdo pure la sũma nel cãpo i da
re e hauere che deue battere para.E poi ala prita del cauedale i dare dirai.cauedale die dar
a di zc.p .p e danno. p danno sedro posto in quella al die hauere p saldo suo val a carti zc.
$.§.f.g° p.zc. E cosi sene fosse sedro vtile. cõ serebbe q̃do qlla del .p e danno se retrouasse piu
i hauere che i dare aloza sugiõgiarresti al dare p saldo ql tanto chiamãdo el cauedale ale car
ti suoi zc.e alui la portesti i hauere issiemi cõ lastre robbe mobili e stabil.e di nuouo i qsto ca
uedal qlle cõuiẽ eẽre sẽpre lultĩ.prita õ tutti liqderni.porrai sẽpre cognoscere tutta tua facul
ta.giõgnẽdo li debiti e crediti che in lib°. A. portasti zc.E qsta del cauedal dcl qderno. cro
ci saldarai ancora.E portarala cõe laltre nel qderno. A. in resto e sũma o voi a prita p pri
ta che lo poi anche fare.ma si costuma farla in sũma pche 1a.volta tutto tuo iuẽtario ape. E
recordate chiamas tue carti.zc.e asserarai poi tutte leprite dl qderno. A.ne lalfabeto ognu
na al suo luogo cõe disopra te dissi.cap° 5°. Acio sẽpe possi cõ facilita trouare le tue facẽde
secondo loro occurençe e cosi fia saldo tutto el primo quaderno con suo giornale e memori
ale. E acio sia piu chiaro de ditto saldo.farai questo altro scontro.Cioe summarai in vn fo
glio tutto eldare del quaderno.croci.E ponlo a man sinistra.E summarai tutto suo hauere
E põlo aman dextra. E poi queste vltime summe resummarai. E farane de tutte quelle
del darvna sũma che si chiamara sũma sũmarũ.E cosi farai vna sũma õ tutte qlle dalauef
che si chiamara ancora lei vna sũmasũmarũ.Oha lap2. sira sũma summarũ.del darc e la fa
si chiama summasũmarũ de lo hauere.Or se qste voi sũme summarũ sirã pare.cioe che tan
to sia luna qto laltra.v3 qlla del dare.e qlla delo hauere.arguirai el tuo qderno eẽre bẽ gui
dato tenuto e saldato p la cagiõe cõ di sopra nel cap° 14.fo detto.Oha se luna õ ditte sum
me summarũ auançasse laltra denotarebbe erronel tuo quaderno.el qual poi con diligẽtia
ti cõuerra trouarlo cõ la industria õlo irelletto che dio te ha dato.e cõ lartefitio dele ragio
ni che harai bene inparato.laqual pte cõe nel pricipio dcl pñte dicẽmo e summamẽte neces
saria albon mercatante altramente non siando bon ragioneri ncli soi fatti andara a rastõi
cõe ciecho. E porzalline sedre molto dãno.adonca cõ ogni studio e cura sforçarati sopra tut
to eẽre buon ragioneri dcd modo a tua cõmodita in qsta sublima opa a pieno a tua bastan
ça.te lo dato con tutte sue regole a tutti suo luoghi debitamente poste.si cõe tutto facilmẽte
per la tauola nel pricipio di qsta opera posta porrai trouare.E ancora p le cose dette q̃ se
quente cõme disopra nel cap°.12° te .pmissi a piu tuo recordo faro 1°.epilogo.cioe sumaria
recolta cẽniale de tutto el pñte trattato.che molto sença dubio te fia vtile. E p me recorda i
rati laltissimo pgare che a suc laude e gloria.Io possa de bene i meglio opãdo .pcedere zc.

Del modo e ordine asap tener le scripture menute cõe sõno scritti de mano lettere fami
liari police.pccisti snie e altri istrumẽti e del registro de le lfe.iportãti. Ca° 35
E quita el modo e ordine de saper tener le scripture e chiarecçe menute comme
sonno scritti de mano de pagamenti facti quietançe de cambi.de robbe datc.let
tere familiari.quali cose sonno fra mercãnti de grãdissima stima.e molta impor

138

tança.e de gran pericolo in perderle e smarrirle.E prima.dele lettere familiari quali spesso fra te e li toi auctori possano acadere. queste sepre stendi e serba in vn banchetto ala fin del mese.E finito elmese legale in vn maço.e ripolle dapte segnando ogniuna defore cioe che la receui el di che li respondi .E cosi si fa amese p mese.E poi ala fin de lanno de tutti qlti maçi farai vn maço grade e luoga e segna suo MD. E qdo poi alcuna lra a ql ricorri. hauerai i tuo studio overo scritoio vna tasca.nela ql reporrai lre cb liamici te deffero cb tu cō letuoi mandasse aloza.sedici che lamandi a roma. mettila in tasca di roma.e se a firença in qlla deffi rença 7c.E poi nel spaciare del sante pigliale con le tuoi al tuo respodente in quel tal luogo lemanda.pcbe el scriure sempre e buono.e anche sufa dar suo beueragio per cer scruito 7c. atorno esso cinta copcira cōe si fa i piu taschette.cioe in tante cpte sonno le terre e luogbi in le quali fai le toe facede cōe diciamo.Roma. Fireçe: Napoli. Milano. Zenoa. Lion. Lodra Bruça 7c.E sopra dicte taschette p ordine scriuerai ilsuo nome.cioe a luna dirai Roma.alal tra. Fireça 7c.in le quali poi reporrai le lre che p qlli luogbi te fossero mandate da qualcb aico che lamandasse.E fatta che li barai respota e mandata.pure in ditta lra de sora. cōe festi del suo receuere.e p cbi.E cosi similiter porrai menzione de la respcsta. E pcbi la mandasti con lo suo giozno.El qual di mai in alcua.tua facenda fa cbe macbi. o piccola o grade cb la sia marime in lre in le qli sepre si deue porre ilmilesimo el di.e luogo.el nome tuo elqual no me si costuma mettarlo da pede aman dextra de la lra in vn cátone.el DP. cō lo di e luogo fra mercatan ti se usa ponere disopra nel principio dela lra.Lra p.a modo bon xpiano ba rai sepre amete de ponere el glozioso nome de nra salute.cioe el doci nome de Jhu.overo in suo scabio la figura de la sca croci.nel cui nome sep tutte le nre opationi debano eer prinzi piate. E farai cosi.croci. 1494.a di. 17.aprile i vinegia. E poi seqta tuo dire. cioe carissimo 7c. ma li studiari e altre genti cōe sonno religiosi 7c.che non traficano. usano nel luogo de ue lalettera e fatta poner di sotto con lo di e DP. e li mercati costumano disopra a modo ditto alt.mente non vi ponendo el di scrcbe confusione. E di te feria fatto besse pcbe seoid la lra che non ba el di notato cbe le fatta de notte. E qlla cbe non a notata.el luogo se uid cbe le fatta i laltr.modo.e non in qsto.e oltra le besse cbe pegio e ne seque segndalo vt vici. Expedita cbe barai sua resposta.poscia al deputato luogo la poni cōe bai inteso.E qsto cbe ditto babiamo de v.sola credilo p tutte. Unde e ancoza danotare cbe qdo le lre che tu ma di fossero de ipotança.qlle tale se vogliano p.a registrarle in vn libro da pte solo a qsto dpu tato.nel ql registro si deue ponere la lra de verbo ad verbū.seila sia ò grande ipotaça cōe sonno lre de cambio.o de robe mandate o ò. 7c.o vero re gistrare solo la substança.cōe me moziale vicēdo i qsto to 7c.babiamo scritto alrale 7c.cioe plo tale 7c.kinmandamo le tal co se 7c.fo p ib.fra de ò tanti 7c.ci cōmise e ricbiede 7c.la qual ponemo in tasca 7c. E di fuore sigilata cbe barai la tua cbe madi e fatto la sopra scritta sufa. p molti ponerui el suo segno di fuore.acio si cognosca cbe sia de mercanti.a iquali molto se deue bauere riguardo. p cbe son qlli cōe i pricipio di qsto trattato vicēmo cbe mantēgano le repub. E a qsto fine de reue uerentia el simile li Rm.Cardinali.pongano defore elloro distito nome.acio niu se possi scu sare de non sape de cbi la fosse. E molto piu aptamete el sancto padre fa le sue patētcmēte apte cōe sōno bolle breuilegi 7c. Auēga cbe alcune cose piu irrisedcbe.poga sotto el sigillo di pescatore 7c.Leqli lre poi a mese p mese o vero anno p anno recozzai i maçgi. overo filçe e da pte le poni ordinatamēte i vno armaro.o sularetto.lecuro.cōe nascano ala çornata co si lasetta.acio possi piu psto a tue occurēçe retrouarle ò laqlcosa.nò curo piu dire pcb io sba stança mal inteso 7c.   Scritti de mano nò pagati de tuoi debitozi cōme te accēnai disopra nel cap°.17.seruarai in vn altro luogo piu secreto cōe son caffi e scatole priliate 7c.E leqtà çe similiter.serua in luogo lecuro p ogni respecto.Ma qdo tu pagasse tu ad altri elriceuere faralo scriuere i i lo libretto de pagamēti cōe in pricipio te dirr.acio nò si possa cosi facilmē smarire e pdere.E cosi obseruarai de le polliçe cbe ipoztano. cōe sōno notole de sensaria ò mercati.o de pesadozi o bolette ò robbe misse o tratte de dogane damiare o da vtra e sctēçe o cartuline de cosoli o altri officij o altri istrumēti de notari i pgamena qli se debano repor re i vn luogo da pte. E cosi copie scritture e pcessi delitre de pcuratozi. E auocati. E similmē te e buono bauere vn libr°.separato piu recozdi cbe si cbiami recozdāçe nel ql ala çornata farai le tue memozie dele cose.cbe dubitasse nò recozdarte.cbe te pozie tornar dāno.nel ql ogni ò al manco la sera nançe vadi adozmire darai ocbio.se cosa fosse da spedire o dafare cbe non fusse expedita 7c.alaql spaçata darai de pēna. E cosi q farai memozia de cose cbe al uicino e amico p vno o doi di pstasse cōe sonno vasa de boregga caldare e altri ordigni 7c. E quel ſimili documéti con gli altri vtiliſſimi ſopra dati reporrai ꝛč.piu e máco çonçando eſiminu endo ſo luoglxi e tṕi a te per tuo.ingegno parcra.pero cħ non e poſſibile apieno de tutto a ponto pér ponto i mercátua dare norma.e notitia pocħ cóme altre uolte ſe dittovol piu póti afare 1? mercatáte cħe un dottore deleggi.Ideo ꝛč.Coſe cħ finora ſóno dette.ſe bñ lapréde rai ſon certo i tutte tue facéde bñ te reggiarai.mediáte el tuo peregrino ingegno ꝛč.

Sum nario de regole E modi ſopra il tenere vno libro di mercanti. Cap°. 36.

Tutti li creditori ſi debono mettere al libro vala tua mano deſtra.E li debitori vala tua mano ſiniſtra. Tutte le ptite cħe ſe metteno allib? hano a eére doppie:cioe ſe tu fai vno cre ditore al ſi fare 1°.debitore.Ciaſcũa prita coſi i vare cóe i ħere ởbbe cóttenere iſe.ꝛcoſe cioe il giorno del pagaméto.La ſóma del pagaméto.E la cagióe del pagaméto. Lultimo nome vela prita vel vebito vebbe eére il prio vella prita vel credito. In ꝗllo medeſimo giorno cħe e ſcritta la prita del debito.i ꝗllo medeſimo giorno vebbe eére ꝗlla vel credito.

Lo bilancio del lib? ſintéde 1? foglio piegato p lo lógo ſul ꝗe vala mano veſtra ſi copiáo li creditori del lib°.e vala ſiniſtra li debitori.E vedeſe ſe laſuma vel vare e ꝗ̃to ꝗlla de laue re.E allora il lib°.ſta bene. El bilaucio del libro vebbe eére pari.cioe cħe tanto vebbe eér la ſuma non dico de creditori.ne vebitori.Ma dico la ſuma vel credito ꝗ̃to la ſuma vel ve bito.E nó eéndo ſaria errore nel libro. El conto di caſſa conuiene cħe ſépre ſia vebitrice. overaméte pari.E ſe altriméte fuſſe ſaria errore nellibro. Non ſi vebbe e non ſipuo fare 1°.vebitore al libro ſença licéça e uolúta vi ꝗllo tale cħa aeére vebitore e ſe pure ſi faceſſe ꝗl la ſcrittura ſeria falſa. Ne ſimilméte non ſi puo porre neppati ne conditioni a. 1? credito ſe ça licéça e volonta del creditore. E ſe pure ſi faceſſe ꝗllaſcrittura ſaria falſa. El lib°.conuie ne cħe ſia tutto tratto fuori a 1°.medeſima móeta.Ma détro poi bñ noiare ꝗllo cħ a cadeſ ſe o vuč.o §.o fioꝛni.o ſcudi voro.o ꝗllo cħe fuſſi Ma nel trarre fuori conuiene cħe ſia tut to a 1°.medeſima moneta cóe priccipiaſti illib°.coſi conuiene ſeguire. La prita vel vebito. o vel credito cħe ſi fa i conto de caſſa ſi puo abreuiare cħi vuole.cioe ſença vire lacagione ſo lamére vire va tale vi tale.ó a tale vi tale.pcħe la cagione ſi uiene a vichiarar nella prita op poſita. Hauédo a fare 1°.cóto nuouo ſi vebbe ſcriuere i'carta noua ſença tornare adietro an cora cħ a vrietro vi trouaſſi ſpacio va metterla.Non ſi vie ſcriuere idrietro.Ma ſépre auá ti per ordine cóevanno li giorni vel tṕo cħe mai non ritornano indrieto. E ſe pure ſi faceſſe ſaria va reputare ꝗllo libro falſo. Se 1°.partita foſſe alibro meſſa per errore cħe non do ueſſi eére cóe adulene ale volte per iſmemoragine e tu la uoleſſi iſtornare farai coſi ſengna ꝗlla tale partita in margine vuna croci o vuna. ħ. E dipoi ſcriui 1°.prita alincontro.cioe a lo oppoſito di ꝗlla nel medeſimo conto.cioe ſela partita errata fuſſe creditricc.poniamo vi § 50ß10ở6.E tu la farai vebitrice.E diraſ e de dare.§ 50.ß10ở6.ſonno per la partita di ꝗtro ſegnata croci cħe ſi ſtorna percħe era errata e non haueua a eére.E ꝗſta partita ſegna la. croc cóe e laltra e ở fatta. Quando loſpacio duno cóto fuſſe pieno.in modo cħ nó ul poteſſe mettere piu prite.E tu voleſſi tirare ꝗllo conto unanꝗ́. Fa coſi guarda ꝗllo cħ e il re ſto del ditto conto.cioe ſeli reſta bauere o a darc. Ora poniamo cħe ꝗllo conto reſti bauere § 28ß4ở2.Dicó cħe tu debbi fare 1°. verſo ſoletto vala parte oppoſita ſença mettere gior‑ no.e dirai coſi. E de dare.§ 28ß4ở2.per reſto vi ꝗſto conto poſto bauere in ꝗſto a car.e ở fatto. E lo detto verſo ſi debe ſegnare in margine dauati coſi.cioe iR°. cħe ſignifica reſto cioe cħel detto uerſo non ne debirzice ancór pcħe ſia dala banda del debitore.Ma uiene a eſ ſere traſportato ꝗllo credito per la via del debito.Ora ti cóuiene uolgere carta e andare tá tó auanti cħe truoui 1°.carta nuoua.E qui fare creditore il detto conto.E nominarlo e fa‑ re prita nuoua ſéça metterui il giorno.E dirai coſi tale di tale ở tali de ħere. § 18ß4.ở2.ſó no per reſto duno ſuo conto leuato in ꝗſto a ca. E ꝗſta partita ſi debbi ſegnare in margine coſi. cioe iR°. cħeſignifica reſto.E ſatta.E coſi comme io to moſtro quando ilconto reſta a bauere con ancora bai afare quando reſtaſſi adare.cioe quello cai meſſo dala banda del credito metter vala banda del debito.

Uando el lib? fuſſe tutto pieno o uechio e tu uoleſſi ridullo a 1? alt° li°. nuouo ſa coſi p̃ti cóuiene vedere cħe ſe il tuo lib°. vecchio e ſegnato i ſu lacouerta poni amo p caſo. A. biſogna cħ i ſul lib? nuouo voue lo voi ridurre ſia ſegnato in ſu la couerta. B. pcħe li libi.ve mercanti váno p ordic luno voppo lalt°.Fo le lře velo.a b c ꝛč.E vipoi leuare ilbilancio vel lib° vechio cħe ſia giuſto e parti cóe vebba eſſere e va ꝗllo bilancio copiare tutti li creditori e vebitori i ſul lib°.nuouo tutti p ordine cóe elli ſtáno i ſul bilácio.E fare tutti li vebitori e creditori ciaſcũ va pſe.e laſcia aciaſc? táto ſpatio

q̄to tu arbitri sere a trauagliare cō seco.E i ciascūa prima ocl ocbitoxe bai a oire p tāti resta
adarc al lib°. uechio segnato. B. a car. i ciasciūa pꝛita ocl creditoxe bai a oire p tanti resta
a bauere al lib° vechio segnato. B. a car .E cosi e riducto al libro nuouo.Oxa p cancellaꝛ
il libro uechio ti cōuicne a ciasciūo cōto acceso ispegnerlo cō lo bilancio sopra ouio.cioe se
vno cōto ocl libro uechio sara creditoxe che lonedrai p lo bilancio farailo ocbitoxe e oir u p
tanti resta bauere a q̄sto cōto posto ocbbi bauere al lib°. nouo segnato. B. a.car.E cosi ba
rai ispeto tutto il lib°. uechioxe acceso al lib°.nuouo.E cosi cōmo io to mostro ouno credito
re cosi bai afare ouno ocbitoxe.Saluo che ooue al creditoxe si fa ocbitoxe posto ocbbi ba
uerc E tu bai a fare creditoxe posto ocbbi oare z e facto.

   Casi che apticne amettere al libro oe mercanti.

   Tutti li o.cōtanti che tu ti trouasti che fussiuo tuoi ꝓprii.cioe che bauessi guadagnati i
oiuersi tpi pel passato o che ti fussino stati lassati oa tuoi parēti moxti.o oonati oa q̄lche pꝛi
cipe farai creditoxe te medēmo.E ocbitore cassa. Tutte le gioie e mercantie che fussino
tue ꝓprie che tu bauessi guadagnate.o cō ti fussino stare lassate p testamēto.o che ti fussino
stare oonate.E q̄ste tale cose si vogliono stimare oa p se luna oa lalt°.q̄llo che vagliano a o.
cōtanti.E tante q̄te cose elle sono tante prite fare al lib°.e fare ciascuna ocbitrice e oire p tā
te mi trouo stimare q̄sto oi tanti o.z̄c.Posto medesimo creditoxe i q̄sto a car.E farai credi
toxe il tuo cōto.cioe te medesimo oi ciascūa prita.Ha nota che q̄lle prite sintēde chi nō siē
no māco oi oieci oucati.luna po che le cose minute oi poco valore non simettano al libro.

   Tutte le cose stabile che tu ti trouasti che fussiuo tue ꝓprie cōe sono case possessiōi botte
che bai afare ocbitoxe octta casa e stimare q̄llo che la uale a tua oiscretiōe a o.cōtanti. E fa
ne creditoxe te medēmo al tuo sopra octto cōto. E oipoi fare ocbitore la possessiōe oa pse e
stimarla cōe e oitto e fane creditoxe te medēmo al tuo sopradetto cōto. e cōe nelle regole to
oitto tutte le prite vogliono bēre i loro tre cose.cioe il giorno e la q̄². oela pecūia e la cagiōe.

   Cōpre che tu facessi oi mercantie.o oitbe cosa si fusse p li o.cōtāti ocbbi fare ocbitore q̄lla
tale mercantia o q̄lla tale cosa e creditore la cassa. E se tu oicessi. io lacōprai a o. cōtanti cōe e
oitto.Ha vno banco gli paço p me.o veramēte vno mio amico gli pago p me.IRispodoti
che a ogni modo bai afare ocbitore q̄lla tale mercantia cōe oisopra.o oitto.Ha ooue io r i
oissi farai creditoxe la cassa tu bai afare creditoꝛ q̄l banco.o q̄llo tuo sico eb p te glia pagati.

   Cōpre che tu facessi oi mercantie.o oicbe cosa sia a termine oalcuno tpo ocbi fare oebitore q̄lla tale mercantia e creditore colui oa cui tu lai cōprata p q̄llo tpo. Cōpre che tu
facessi oi mercantia.o oicbe cosa si sia a pte o.e pte tpo ocbbi fare ocbitore q̄lla tale mercancia E creditore colui oa cui tu lai cōprata p q̄llo tpo cō q̄sti patti che li babbi bauere oiciamo
il terço oi o.cōtāti E loresto fra sci mesi ꝓximi futuri.E doppo q̄sto fare unaltra prita.cioe
debitore colui oa cui tu lai cōprata oi q̄lla q̄°.oi o.cōtanti che mōta q̄lla terça parte che fu oi
parto oicōtanti E creditore la cassa o q̄llo bancho che glipagasse prc. Tutte le uēdite ch
tu facessi oi mercantie o oaltre cose bai a fare tutto cōme oisopra saluo ebai a mettere plo op
posito.cioe che ooue oisopra ti oissi che sēpre facessi debitore lamercancia:q̄ nelle vēdite bai
a fare sēpre creditore la mercancia E ocbitore cassa se e uēduta a o.cōtanti o ocbitore q̄l banc
co che se li bauesse ꝓmessi E se e vēduta a termine.bai a fare debitore colui acui tu lbai uēdu
ta p q̄llo termine e se fusse uēduta a pre o.e pte tpo bai a fare cōe oisopra ti mostrai nelle cō
pre q̄lle oue prite.. Se tu vēdessi una mercācia abaratto ouiamo. Io bo vēduto libbre mil
le oilana oingbliterra abaratto oi pluere cioe alibre oumilia oi peucre oomando comme
sa a cōtare q̄sta scrittura al lib° fa.cosi ultima q̄llo che vale ilpipe a tua oiscretiōe a o.cōtā
ti.Oꝛ poniamo che tu lo stimi ouc.oodici ilcēto adōq̄ le oumilia libbre vagliono ouc.i40
cōtāti.e po farai creditore lalana o ouc.i40.p q̄to lai venduta E q̄sto modo obsua sēpre i
leprite tutte oli baratti e q̄li seni baurō §.ouamilia oipeucre stimato. :40.ouc.Posto oa
to peucre ocbbi oare i q̄sto a car. E fāne ocbitore ilpcucre. Oanari cōtanti che tu ꝓstassi
a q̄lche tuo amico bai a fare ocbitoꝛ lamico achi tu gli bai ꝓstati e creditore cassa. Se tu
riceuessi o.cōtanti in pistanca oa q̄lche amico bai afare ocbitore cassa e creditore lamico.

   Se tu bauessi ꝓso otto.o oicu.o vēn ouc. p assicurare naue o galee o altra cosa ocbbi fare creditoxe sicurta oi nauilij e cbiarire che e cōe e q̄do e ooue e q̄to p cēto .E debitoxe cōto
oi cassa. Oercantie che ti fussino mandate oa altri cō cōmissione ouēderle o barattarle
oequali tu bauessi bauer la tua puisiōe.Dico che tu ocbbi fare ocbitore al libro q̄lla tale mer
cantia attrnēre al tale o tale p lo pronto o p gabella.o p nolo o p mettere il magazino E cre
ditoxe cōto oi cassa. Tutte le spese oi mercantie oi o.cōtanti che tu farai.o p nolo.o p ga
belle.o vetture o sēsente.o poxtature sa creditore la cassa.E ocbitoxe quella tale mercantie
per laq̄le tu gli bai ispesi.

Casi che acade mettere ale recordançe del mercante.

Utte lemasserizie di casa o di bottega che tu ti truoui. Ma vogliono essere per ordine.cioe tutte le cose di ferro da perse con spatio da potere agiongnere se bi sognasse.E così da segnare in margine quelle che fussino perdute o vendute o donate o guaste.Ma non si intende masserizie minute dipoco valore. E fare ri cordo di tutte le cose dottone da perse comme e vetro. E simile tutte le cose distagno . E si mile tutte lecose dilengno. E così tutte le cose dirame.E così tutte le cose dariento e doro ℈c. Sempre con spatio di qualche carta da potere arrogere se bisognasse.e così dadare notitia di quello che mancasse. Tutte lemalleuerie o obbzighi o promesse che promettessi per ql che amico. e chiarire bene che e comme. Tutte lemercantie o altre cose che ti fossino laf sate i guardia o a serbo oi pistança da qlche amico.e così tutte lecose ch tu pistassi'a altri tuoi amici. Tutti limercati conditionati cioe copre ovedite cóme p ereplovno cótrato cioe d tu mi mandi con leproffime galee che torneranno dingbluerra tanti cantara di lane ossimi stri a caso che le fieno buone e recipienti. Io ti daro tanto del cantaro o del cento o veramē te ti mandaro alincontro tanti cantara di cottoni. Tutte le case o possessioni o botteghe o gioie che tu affitassi a tanti duc.o a tante lire lanno.E quando tu ricoterai ilfitto aloza dl lroinari fanno a mettere al libro comme disopra ti diffi. Prestando qualche gioia o uasella menti dariento o doro a qualche tuo amico per otto o quidici giorni diqueste tale cose no si mettono al libro.ma sene fa ricordo ale ricordançe.perche fra pochi giorni lai bariauere. E così per contra se a te fossi prestato simili cose non li debbi mettere al libro.Ma farne me morza ale ricordançe perche presto lai a rendere.

Comme si scriuono lire e soldi e danari picioli e altre abreuiature.

Lire soldi danari picioli libbre once danarpesi grani carati ducati fiorin larghi.

℔ ₰ ð p̄ libbre ℔ ðp g°. ҟ duc. fio.lar

<table>
<tr><td>

MCCCC° Lxxxxiiij°.
Lodouico dipiero forestai vedare a di.iiij.nouembre. 1493.℔.44.ₛ.i:ð.8.porto contati in pistaça.posto caf sa auere.a car. 2
E a di.18.detto ℔.18.ₛ.11.ð. 6.promettemo a lui a marti no dipiero foraboschi asuo piacere posto bēre i qsto.a c.2.

Casa i mano di simone da leffo bóbeni de daf adi.14. nouèbre 1493.℔.62.ₛ.13. ð.2.da francesco dantonio caualcanti in qsto a c.2

Martino di piero fora bo schi de dare a di.20.nouem bre.1493.℔.18.ₛ.11.ð.6.por to luimedesimo contadi po sto cassa a car. 2.

Francesco dantonio caual cáti de dare a di.12.di noué bre.1493.℔.20.ₛ.4.ð.2.cl.p misse anostro piaceī pl lodo uico di pierosoreftai a c.2.

</td><td>

℔ 44 ₛ 8.

℔ 18 ₛ11 ð6.

℔ 62 ₛ13 ð6.

℔ 18 ₛ11 ð6.

℔ 20 ₛ4 ð2.

</td><td>

MCCCC° Lxxxxiiij.
Lodouico dipiero forestai de bauere a di.22.nouébre 1493.℔.20.ₛ.4.ð.2.sóno p parte di pagamento.E per lui cetia promissi a nostro piacere fracescho dátonio. caualcáti posto dare a c. 2.℔

Casa in mano di simone daleffo bóbeni de bauere a di.14.nouèbre.1493.℔.44. ₛ.1.ð.8.alo douico di piero forestani in qsto. a car. 2. ℔
E a di.22.nouembre.1493 ℔.18.ₛ.11.ð.6.a martino di piero foraboschi.a ca. 2. ℔

Martino di piero fora bo schidi bauere a di.18.noué bre.1493.℔.18.ₛ.11.ð.6.gli pmettemo a suo piacere p lodouico di piero forestani posto obbi bēre i qsto a c.2.℔

Francescho dátonio caual canti de bauere a di.14.no uébre.1493.℔.62.ₛ.13.ð.6. reco lui medesimo ptáti po sto cassa dare a.car.2.

</td><td>

20 ₛ4 ð2.

44 ₛ11 ð8.

18 ₛ11 ð6.

18 ₛ11 ð6.

℔ 62 ₛ13 ð6.

</td></tr>
</table>

Bibliography

Books

Brown, Richard. HISTORY OF ACCOUNTING AND ACCOUNTANTS, Edinburgh: T. C. and E. C. Jack, 1905.

Crivelli, Pietro. ORIGINAL TRANSLATION OF THE TREATISE ON DOUBLE ENTRY BOOKKEEPING BY LUCAS PACIOLI, London: Institute of Bookkeepers, Ltd. 1924.

de Roover, Raymond. "The Development of Accounting Prior to Luca Pacioli According to the Account-Books of Medieval Merchants," in A. C. Littleton and B. Yamey, STUDIES IN THE HISTORY OF ACCOUNTING, Homewood: Richard D. Irwin, Inc. 1956.

Edler, Florence (now Mrs. de Roover). GLOSSARY OF MEDIEVAL TERMS IN BUSINESS. ITALIAN SERIES, Cambridge: Medieval Academy of America, 1931.

Eldridge, H. J. as revised by Leonard Frankland. THE EVOLUTION OF THE SCIENCE OF BOOKKEEPING, 2d edition, London: Gee & Company, Ltd., 1954.

Geijsbeek, John B. ANCIENT DOUBLE ENTRY BOOKKEEPING, Denver: John B. Geijsbeek, 1914.

Littleton, A. C. ACCOUNTING EVOLUTION TO 1900, New York: American Institute Publishing Company, 1933.

Peragallo, Edward. ORIGIN AND EVOLUTION OF DOUBLE ENTRY BOOKKEEPING, New York: American Institute Publishing Company, 1938.

Taylor, R. Emmett. NO ROYAL ROAD: LUCA PACIOLI AND HIS TIMES, Chapel Hill: University of North Carolina Press, 1942.

——. "Luca Pacioli," in A. C. Littleton and B. Yamey, STUDIES IN THE HISTORY OF ACCOUNTING, Homewood: Richard D. Irwin Inc., 1956.

Woolf, A. H. A SHORT HISTORY OF ACCOUNTANTS AND ACCOUNTANCY, London: Gee & Company, Ltd. 1912.

Articles and Other Publications

Anonymous, A review of ANCIENT DOUBLE-ENTRY by John B. Geijsbeek, JOURNAL OF ACCOUNTING, November 1914, p. 404-5.

Bonrey, Alfred, "The Name of Paciolo," THE ACCOUNTING REVIEW, July 1943, p. 205-9.

Crivelli, Pietro, "Paciolo on Double Entry Bookkeeping, An Original Translation," ACCOUNTANT, January 1925.

de Roover, Raymond, "Paciolo or Pacioli," ACCOUNTING REVIEW, January 1944, p. 58-9; also in April 1944, p. 193.

Fitzpatrick, R. J., "Paciolo—Father of Accounting," KENTUCKY ACCOUNTANT, March-April 1952, p. 6.

Hatfield, Henry Rand, A review of the translation of Paciolo by Pietro Crivelli, JOURNAL OF ACCOUNTANCY, April 1925, p. 74.

——, "An Historical Defense of Bookkeeping," JOURNAL OF ACCOUNTANCY, April 1924, p. 241-253.

Langer, Clarence, "Paciolo: Patriarch of Accounting," ACCOUNTING REVIEW, July 1958, p. 482-4.

Taylor, R. Emmett, "The Name of Pacioli," ACCOUNTING REVIEW, January 1944, p. 69-76.

Thompson, H. W. and B. S. Yamey, "Bibliography of Bookkeeping and Accounts," London, The Institute of Chartered Accountants in England and Wales, no date.

144

For Product Safety Concerns and Information please contact our EU
representative GPSR@taylorandfrancis.com
Taylor & Francis Verlag GmbH, Kaufingerstraße 24, 80331 München, Germany